The purpose of this collection is to provide the student with an introduction to the way in which the discipline of economics tackles the problems posed in affluent societies by their various 'waste' products. 'Pollution economics' introduces a student to aspects of price economics, public finance, and political economy in relation to a pressing and complex public concern. The work includes a number of Canadian statements on pollution and its control in this country, and gives the text of two recent pieces of legislation on the topic.

The selections in this volume present a wide variety of opinions, ideas, and facts about the economic dimension of the ecological crisis. Pollution costs money – pollution abatement also costs money and these costs will have to be paid somehow by some people. The contributors – politicians, businessmen, and professors – explore the problem of pollution and its control as each sees it, and the volume as a whole should help encourage a greater awareness both of economics as a way of thinking and of the difficulties in making the right public policies.

Economic thinking and pollution problems

Economic thinking and pollution problems

Edited by D.A.L. AULD

University of Toronto Press

© University of Toronto Press 1972

Toronto and Buffalo

ISBN 0-8020-1766-5 (casebound)

ISBN 0-8020-1767-3 (paperback)

ISBN 0-8020-0044-4 (microfiche)

LC 75 151353

Printed in Canada

Preface

Water and air pollution cost money. Soot and dirt particles from a variety of sources send our cleaning bills soaring. These particles and various unseen gases or vapours contribute to a deterioration of health, resulting in high medical bills for the treatment of bronchitis, emphysema, and other respiratory diseases. Pollution of water forces communities to spend thousands, perhaps millions, of dollars on equipment and supplies to render water drinkable. Industries which need clean water for production processes are faced with rising costs of cleansing filthy water. Cottage-owners find that the value of their property plummets when their lake is classified unsafe for swimming.

Pollution abatement also costs money. The price of an automobile rises when we decide to reduce exhaust pollution by installing afterburners. The installation of smoke precipitators in factories contributes to the costs of production and conceivably increases the price of the product to the consumer. To prevent oil spillage, tanker ships must be fitted with costly equipment. Cities must construct modern primary and secondary sewage treatment facilities to prevent the pollution of rivers and lakes.

In order that we can make sensible judgments and decisions about pollution levels and control, it is helpful to have as much knowledge about the subject as possible. The purpose of this book is to make a contribution towards that knowledge by presenting to the reader a variety of ideas, opinions, and facts about some of the economic and financial aspects of pollution. The contributors to this volume range from politicians to company presidents. The book is directed towards politicians, businessmen, students, and anyone interested in acquainting himself with these aspects of the pollution problem. For those who are interested in a more formal analysis of the economics of pollution, I would recommend "On the Theory of Optimum Externality," by F.T. Dolbear, Jr., *American Economic Review*, March 1967, and "Production, Consumption, and Externalities," by R.U. Ayres and A.V. Kneese, *American Economic Review*, June 1969.

In the final preparation of this work, I have received helpful advice from Rik Davidson, the social science editor at the University of Toronto Press. I should like to thank those authors, editors, and publishers who gave permission to reprint the selections; details about their original appearance are given in the introductions to each article. I am grateful for the comments of those students of the University of Guelph who attended my course in the fall of 1969 on "Pollution Economics."

D.A.L. AULD

Contents

4 Broader conceptual approaches

5 Appendices

Part 1

Pollution as an economic problem

An economic analysis of environmental pollution

In this first selection, the editor outlines briefly some of the economic reasons why environmental pollution has recently reached such serious proportions. The free-enterprise, market economy has not operated to ration the resources of air and water and this has led to their misuse and destruction. Economic thinking can be helpful in finding solutions to the problem of pollution. This paper is a shortened version of a seminar address presented to the Centre for Resources Development at the University of Guelph in 1969.

Scientifically, pollution of water, air, and land occurs when foreign material is added to the natural environment in such quantities or at such a rate that the environment can no longer support this material without an appreciable alteration in nature itself. Is this a matter for economics, the study of how man satisfies his wants? For two reasons the answer must surely be an emphatic yes. First, economic activities have been and are involved in creating environmental pollution. Second, economic thinking can be useful in analysing the problem, assisting in the preparation of abatement solutions, and in curtailing future possible pollution.

Mankind, to a considerable extent, satisfies his wants or desires through material consumption. Most of this consumption is in the form of goods which are produced in processes using air, water, or both as factors of production. It would appear from what has happened to air, water, and perhaps land that these resources have been utilized in a rather careless manner. In fact, many would argue that air and water have been more seriously mismanaged than any other resource.

One of the major reasons for the disregard of these resources stems from the fact that they have not been regarded as economic goods — that is, goods which are relatively scarce. The use-value of both air and water has always, of course, been recognized, but the apparently endless supply made them "free." This seeming abundance and the particular physical characteristics of water and air made it difficult to invest in them any property rights, either private or public. True, there is a substantial body of international law dealing with water as it pertains to a country's sovereignty. And within some countries, laws and regulations exist with respect to stream or river rights. However, the extent to which regulations cover the use of air and water and their quality is limited. Where laws have existed in Canada, their administration and prosecution have, until recently, been weak and sporadic, partly because of an unwillingness on society's part to devote funds to this purpose.

Let us examine first of all, the relationship between production and pollution.[1] The basic aim of any non-monopolist producer, whether an entrepreneur in a capitalistic economy or plant manager in a socialist economy, is to maximize output or profit through efficient utilization of resources used in the production.

Regardless of the degree of efficiency, however, most production processes involve some amount of waste, and it is this waste which causes pollution of the air or water. Total use of all wastes to produce economic goods would be one method of arresting pollution, but this kind of production efficiency is some distance in the future. However, some success has recently been achieved with such recycling – for example, the use of gaseous waste from smelter operations to produce fertilizers.

The disposal of waste products is an integral step in the production process. If the disposal of wastes becomes expensive for the firm or plant, solutions will be sought to reduce wastes or convert them into economic products. On the other hand, if disposal costs remain zero, no such incentive exists unless, of course, the waste can be transformed into a profit-making product. Looking at costs to the firm or plant itself, we can illustrate this as follows.

If disposal costs (D_w) equal zero, then the firm or plant will convert its waste into economic products as long as

$$(1) \qquad W.C_w \qquad < \qquad P_w.W_t \qquad [D_w \quad = \quad 0],$$

where

$$
\begin{aligned}
W &= \text{waste products (quantity)} \\
C_w &= \text{per unit cost of converting waste product} \\
P_w &= \text{per unit selling price of converted waste} \\
W_t &= \text{converted waste product.}
\end{aligned}
$$

Even if the disposal costs are greater than zero, it would still be economical for the firm to convert the waste as long as

$$(2) \qquad (W.C_w \quad - \quad P_w.W_t) \qquad < \quad D_w \qquad [D_w \quad > \quad 0].$$

It must be remembered that (1) and (2) represent situations as seen by the firm in the light of profit maximization. If we were to add the social costs of pollution, E_w, the above relationship is modified such that from the social viewpoint, treatment of waste products or pollutants should be undertaken when

$$(3) \qquad (W.C_w \quad - \quad P_w.W_t) \qquad < \quad D_w + E_w.$$

Suppose

$$
\begin{aligned}
D_w &= \$\ 31{,}000 \\
E_w &= \$100{,}000 \\
W.C_w &= \$120{,}000 \\
P_w.W_t &= \$\ 90{,}000.
\end{aligned}
$$

From the firm's point of view (see 2), and of course society's (see 3), it is worthwhile to treat the pollutants. However, if $D_w = \$29{,}000$ then it will not be worthwhile from the firm's point of view to convert waste, even though it remains worthwhile to do so from society's point of view.

Historically, disposal costs have been close or equal to zero, and because of this there was little incentive to treat waste material. Air and water, the convenient avenues of waste disposal, were zero-priced as far as the firm was concerned. In addition, there was little interest or immediate reason to be concerned about the external effects of waste disposal. After all, water and air were free goods, available in endless supply and apparently able to absorb the waste products to an acceptable degree. Thus, the only situation in which waste was treated and sold as a different product was that described by (1) above.

The above discussion considered industrial pollution, but automobile pollution or municipal sewage disposal can be used equally well as examples. For the municipality, the objective is to dispose of waste in the cheapest manner. Providing there are no external effects on the area immediately about the waste-disposing municipality, E_w and D_w are close or equal to zero. Automobile manufacturers have always been aware that the internal combustion engine produced a toxic waste gas, but with the existing small disposal costs and little awareness of external costs, there was no reason for the development and installation of exhaust afterburners. Without government regulation, firms would find it profitable to install such devices only if consumers demanded them (and, of course, paid for them). However, we are coming to realize that the external costs are likely very high in terms of disease and health costs. Even if D_w and $P_w.W_t$ are zero, there is increasing evidence to suggest that $E_w > W.C_w$, indicating that, from society's viewpoint, afterburners on internal combustion engines are necessary.

In retrospect, one might argue that if law and economics had given more attention to the ownership, use, and future opportunity costs of air and water, the pollution story would be quite different. Even recently published textbooks in economics give only a brief consideration to this question, several still referring to air as a free good. A good may be considered free now because of its abundance, but it could be economic (scarce) in fifty years. The point should also be made that a good which appears free to an individual may be scarce to society. By establishing now that a good is free may hamper efforts to change its legal status as the good becomes scarce.

The physical nature of air and water have, in part, contributed to the problem of maintaining their quality in a free-enterprise economy. For example, air is what we would call a collective good — no one can be excluded from consuming it. Consequently, there can be no private air market in which individuals express their preference for clean air by purchasing certain quantities at a price. Without a market for air, an individual is rather helpless in promoting efficient use of this resource.

It is worthwhile, also, to reflect briefly upon what might have occurred if air and water had been treated as goods requiring collective action, when waste disposal was involved.[2] One possibility would have been to place these resources under the direction or trusteeship of government. This would not, of course, guarantee optimal resource use, but at least there would have been more collective decision-making about their use. Even if it were possible, private ownership of such a scarce factor as clean air might not produce optimal resource allocation; a "free-enterprise" person would hold out for as long as he could in an attempt to get a high price for his share of air. Since no production could commence until everyone (in an area) sold his air rights, it is possible that no production would take place even though it was socially desirable. If the government charged users according to volume or toxicity of wastes placed in the water or air, technology would have developed the means of reducing pollutants or the prices of products would have reflected the cost of these resources. Another option, that of strict quality regulation, would have forced producers to eliminate pollutants or cease production. Either of these latter courses would have resulted in products priced higher than if air and water were free. Such pricing practices would have led to a greater degree of rationing of the amount of air and water used for waste disposal.

The combination of no market and unrestricted property rights for air and water has not been the cause of pollution. Rather, the existence of these facts in the face of rapid technological developments and urbanization has accelerated the reduction in the quality of the environment. At the heart of the matter is the economic process, and an understanding of the economics involved can help us to arrive at rational policies which will maintain a more desired balance between the environment and the output of goods and services. Economics can help, but the actual reduction of pollution will also involve consideration in other areas of study such as biochemistry, geography, and political science. The market economy was devised by man to serve his purpose — it can be altered to attain new objectives in a changing environment.

One of the most important contributions of economics to finding solutions to the problem of pollution is to quantify the social costs of pollution. These social costs include the expentitures needed to render the polluted resource fit for use, the expenditures made to avoid pollution effects, plus the damages inflicted upon society by the wastes themselves. The corrective part of pollution costs is not difficult to quantify as it is simply the expenditures made by individual or public authorities to purify water or air. For example, how much does it cost industry x to purify the polluted water it needs in its production process? Avoidance costs are also measurable in terms of such expenditures as air-conditioning equipment or movement away from the polluted area. Estimating the cost of the damages caused by pollution is the more difficult task. However, if we are to place a price on air and water, an estimate of these costs is necessary since it can be used to derive a market value for these resources. The purpose here is to examine briefly what these costs are, how they can be measured, and the validity of such cost estimates.

In the case of water pollution, the damages created are, to the economist, largely in terms of disappearing fishing industries and the slow destruction of present or future recreational areas. Losses to fishing can be estimated by examining the statistics that reveal declining catches in a polluted area. But there is more than just a lost income source. For some areas, it is a loss of a way of life to people who have known only fishing. It means welfare, social upheaval, and other associated disutilities to which money costs cannot be imputed. Recreation losses can, in some cases, be measured, but in many instances it means a personal loss when a lake or river is closed to fishing, swimming, or boating. The value of this sort of loss cannot be readily ascertained and in traditional economic and governmental thought has been all but ignored.

Air pollution damages are manifold. Scientific and medical evidence at present indicates that such diseases as emphysema, bronchitis, tuberculosis, and the common cold are precipitated or at least made more acute by the presence of pollutants in the atmosphere. How do we evaluate, in dollar terms, the premature deaths caused by diseases that are accelerated because of polluted air? To what extent do hospital, medical, and drug expenditures in large cities depend on pollution-induced sicknesses? There are techniques for estimating such losses and some progress has been made in this type of measurement. Along with health costs, polluted air often means more expenditure on cleaning and painting. These are the corrective or avoidance costs that are involved with pollution. An estimate of additional cleaning costs resulting from pollution in one large US city is as high as two hundred dollars per capita. Then there are the immeasurable costs such as not being able to see clear blue sky because of smog.

For too long now, economics has regarded the social costs of consumption and production as interesting but only special aberrations of the price system. Unfortunately this is not so — these costs, in the form of environmental pollution, are widespread and must be recognized as such. The contribution that economics can make to solving problems of pollution is threefold. First, it can provide the analytical framework wherein the problem can be clearly defined. Second, the applications of benefit-cost analysis discussed later in this volume are extremely useful in identifying all the returns and outlays (non-financial included) associated with abatement programs. Finally, in divising control and management programs, the economist can evaluate their efficiency and comment on the distributional aspects which these programs may embody.

NOTES

1   For a more detailed analysis of this relationship, see J.H. Dales, *Pollution, Property and Prices* (Toronto: University of Toronto Press, 1968).
2   Water, more than air, has been subjected to collective action involving hydro power, irrigation, etc. But only in the case of municipal water supplies has there been any concerted attempt to deal with the waste problem.

Tools for analysing some environmental problems

This is a selection from a book by A.V. Kneese and O.C. Herfindahl, *Quality of the Environment: An Economic Approach to Some Problems in Using Land, Water and Air* (Washington, DC: Resources for the Future, 1965). The portion included here deals with the question of side-effects from economic activities or what economists refer to as "externalities" or "external diseconomies." The authors define and give an example of externalities, showing how their existence relates to the problem of compensation for pollution damage. They also outline the significance of these effects and make clear that an understanding of externalities is extremely helpful to an understanding of pollution and its control.

Contemporary society is dependent on man's ability to work fundamental changes in the natural environment. Indeed, this society could not exist without large-scale clearing of forested land and plowing of prairies, without substantial changes in natural drainage systems, and without the conversion of rural landscapes into the compact urban places essential for many industrial and commercial processes.

In using resources to produce high and rising levels of income, however, effects are often produced that are incidental to the main purpose. Some of these "side effects," as they might be called, go beyond the economic unit that produces them and may affect others in important ways — some favorably and some unfavorably. Such effects may be thought of as a part of the environment in which we work and produce.

It is obvious that the economy is full of these side effects. Most of them are inconsequential or are unavoidable, for to live in and participate in a society necessarily exposes us to the activities of others in ways that are beyond control — whether our own individual control or the control of society. Some of these effects are easily controllable, however, and the impact of others is so serious that our best effort to ameliorate them is warranted.

To a large extent, individuals or households, rather than businesses, receive the direct effects of these environmental hazards. In the areas of water and air pollution, for example, a good many pollutants directly affect the health of individuals who have had no transaction with the "producer" of the pollutant. Here the flow of stimuli to the affected parties involves the transmission of physical particles.

In other problem areas, however, it is not health as such, but the preferences of individuals which may be affected either directly or by altering the prices of goods and services. Such cases — in which health is not directly affected — may sometimes involve the transmission of physical bodies and sometimes only the flow of visual, aural, or olfactory impressions.

Finally, there are external effects of which the individual may be unaware but which may be of considerable importance to his well-being. One common example is the complex set of stimuli flowing to the individual from his urban environment. Even when the existence of these stimuli is consciously recognized, their effects on the psyche are often very imperfectly perceived by the persons affected.

Admittedly, the two general categories of external effects that have been distinguished here — the "direct" effects on health and those effects that involve preferences — are not completely independent. Individual preferences with respect to health in combination with factors affecting it may differ. And for many people, health itself can be affected by the psychic satisfactions and dissatisfactions they experience. In spite of these considerations, the distinction appears to be an important and useful one, because the means for analyzing and dealing with the two categories are likely to be quite different . . .

While diverse in many respects, the problem areas selected for discussion in this study do have much in common — in origin, diagnosis, and treatment. To see why this is so, we must re-examine some fundamentals of economics to show how the market system operates under two different sets of basic conditions. Let us look at the following two cases:

1. A hypothetical system in which the activities of the different economic units are independent of each other in a "real" sense. That is, a change in the output or activity of a firm (or person) does not *entail* a change in the output of any other firm or in the satisfaction experienced by an individual.

2. A system in which activities of some economic units are partially but not completely independent.

CASE 1. INDEPENDENT ECONOMIC ACTIVITIES

Under certain conditions a market economy will produce precisely those goods and services wanted by consumers, produce these in just the quantities wanted, and produce these quantities in the cheapest possible way. One of the important conditions for this result is that economic activities be independent in a "real" sense. In other words, it is a condition where quantities of *all* parts of an individual's consumption are under his control and *all* the inputs of each business, such as labor, services of machines, etc., are under its control. If we further imagine an economy not disturbed by the introduction of new methods of production or changes in consumer tastes, an economy in which both consumers and producers know what they are doing and in which no industry is dominated by a few firms, we can envision a succession of adjustments which would yield these happy results. Adam Smith, who was perhaps the first to perceive clearly the possibility of an economic system functioning in this way, described the process as the market's "invisible hand." The importance of this perception remains undiminished even today, for it serves to isolate for us and permit us to understand the basic function of a market economy — the organization of production so as to produce what each consumer wants produced within the limit of his income.

Things actually don't work out quite that way, a fact which will surprise no one who is exposed to the day-by-day operations of the economy. In order to construct on paper an abstract model of the economy which will clearly exhibit these properties, it is necessary to imagine a world which is different from the real world. But the automatic functioning of the invisible hand of the market, which can be seen so clearly in this simplified model, becomes obscured when we look at the real world and ask how well the economy succeeds in producing what is wanted. While observers differ on the degree to which the economy falls short in performing this function, all are agreed that it does fall short.

CASE 2. EXTERNALITIES

Some reasons for this less-than-perfect operation of the economy are clear. Technological change and changes in consumer tastes are disturbing factors that can bring problems of adjustment. Consumer or producer ignorance may prevent people from doing as well as they might with the resources at their command. But of equal importance is the fact that what a consumer consumes or what a business firm uses is not entirely within its control. That is, there are flows of some goods or services that come to the consumer or business whether he wants them or not and without his paying for them. This situation may be described by saying that a change in the output of one economic unit (a firm or consumer) necessarily affects the inputs (and hence the output) of some other economic unit. That is, the activities of one economic unit may generate "real" effects that are external to it. These effects are often called external effects, or "externalities." It is exactly this which characterizes each of the problem areas discussed in these pages. For example, an increase in the output of a cannery may increase stream pollution, which in turn will require downstream firms or communities to spend more money to clean up the water they use. They have experienced an unwanted increase of certain inputs — pollutants in this case.

Thus it is evident that the activities of any kind of economic unit, whether a family, a business firm, or a governmental unit, may generate direct, or external, effects on other economic units. The variety of possible cases is very great, and the range of problems and possible solutions is correspondingly great. The number of other economic units affected may vary from one to all in the economy. The damages (or benefits) inflicted may not vary with the output of the initiating unit (damages may be constant) or they may increase in various ways as output of the initiator changes. At one extreme stands a "pure" case, one in which the effects of an economic unit's activity are wholly external to that unit and are available to anyone and everyone. Such effects have come to be called "public goods." Stock examples are certain governmental services such as the provision of defense or the legal system. Such services have the peculiar property that my consumption of them does not diminish yours. Hence it is impractical to get very many people to pay "voluntarily" for their consumption of these services. We therefore voluntarily decide through the political system to require payment in the form of taxes for the support of such services. Some of the cases discussed in this study have something of a public good aspect about them. This complicates their treatment and makes certain remedies impractical.

THE SIGNIFICANCE OF EXTERNAL EFFECTS

If external effects are present, a misallocation of resources is likely to be the result whether the external effect is beneficial or detrimental to its recipient. The reason for this is that the signals which tell a firm how much it should produce — price and cost — may not work properly in the presence of external effects. With no external effects present, we may think of a firm comparing the price it will get from making and selling another unit of its produce with the associated cost. So long as price is greater than this cost, it will pay to expand output. When the two are equal, it will not pay to expand output any further, for that would diminish profit. This output happens also to be the right output from the point of view of the consumers viewed as a group, for the value of the article to them as measured by price is just equal to the costs of making it. These costs are equal to the value of other articles that could have been produced and hence measure what consumers had to give up in order to produce the article in question. If labor services are used to produce shoes, they can't be used to produce furniture.

If external effects are present, this nice balance may be upset. Suppose that a business pollutes a stream and that this increases the costs of treating water supplies downstream. If the business is not induced to take account of this effect, it will neglect these costs in deciding how much to produce. From the point of view of the consumers (again viewed as a group) the firm is producing too much, for the costs associated with the production of another unit of the business' product are now greater than its price. If all costs are taken into account, including the higher water treatment costs, consumers will be giving up other products that could have been produced (the value of which is measured by all costs) in return for a unit of product that is less valuable. This is a misallocation of production. Note that if the external effect had been beneficial the result would also have been a misallocation, but output of the product in question would have been too small rather than too large.

External effects may be generated and received by any pair of economic units. Smith's record player may disturb Jones's rest. Or their cars may slow each other and other drivers on the way to work. We may swim in or picnic alongside water that has been polluted by businesses, individuals, or even governmental units. In the case of the problems discussed here, individuals are important as recipients of the external effects involved.

Misallocation of production – this is the problem that may result when external effects are present. It does not follow, however, that detrimental external effects should be eliminated, for this might entail the elimination of other associated effects or products that are of greater value to consumers. In dealing with the allocation problem arising from external effects, the goal is to find some means whereby decisions on how much to produce take proper account of all the costs and benefits flowing from the economic activity in question. Within a static framework, there are three ways to get this result. One is for the unit(s) that generate(s) the effect to come to agreement with the recipient(s) of the effect on the proper level of the effect — perhaps with a payment from one to the other. Where the effect is measurable and the number of units involved is small, this solution may be feasible.

A second method is to "internalize" the problem so that a single economic unit will take into account all of the costs and benefits associated with the effect. One way is to enlarge the size of the economic unit. For example, the same regional agency might be responsible for both sewage treatment and water supply. Another way to induce consideration of all costs and benefits is to change the limitations under which the initiator of the effect is operating. This could be done by imposing a tax or charge on the effect that is emitted (or a subsidy if the effect is beneficial), in which case the firm may decide to reduce the effect either by cutting the output of its main product or by spending some money to reduce the external effect, for example, by treating waste solutions in the plant. Still another way is to regulate the emission directly. For example, it might be required that an undesirable emission be kept below a certain specified level.

"Internalizing" the problem has the advantage of letting the economic units involved decide on the best adjustment to be made in the light of all costs and benefits. It may be possible and desirable to eliminate or reduce the effect, but there will be some cases in which the best thing to be done is simply to bear it.

A third method is to control production directly, perhaps by governmental operation of the activity that produces the external effect.

In the search for ways to improve the misallocation resulting from external effects, care must always be exercised to take into account any additional costs or penalties associated with the remedy. It is quite possible, for example, to set standards designed to reduce external effects so strict that there will be a loss to national product rather than a gain. Nor should it be assumed that other types of governmental regulations are costless, for they sometimes require large regulatory staffs and may involve other types of costs, some of which are not obvious and may be hard to measure.

There is one other way of dealing with externalities which may be usable in some cases but which goes beyond the static framework in which externalities are usually considered. It may be possible to conceive of new processes or new ways of organizing production so as to reduce or eliminate undesired external effects or to enhance desirable effects. The conception of new processes should be distinguished from different methods of production which are already known but whose use can be induced by, say, the imposition of a tax on the external effect. The distinction between the use of different methods already known and genuinely new methods is hazy both in theory and practice, but it is important to realize that substantial changes in production methods are sometimes possible if a way can be found to focus attention on the problem.

Part 2

Water and air pollution

Standard-setting as a frame of reference

In order for society to make rational judgments about expenditure on air pollution control, it is helpful to know just what are the costs of air pollution. *Economic Costs of Air Pollution* by R.G. Ridker (New York: Frederick Praeger, 1967) is a detailed measurement of health costs associated with air pollution. The first chapter of this book, which is reprinted below, is a general framework for analysing air pollution costs. Although it is not possible to measure all the costs of pollution, the approach outlined here can be of great help in making decisions about the amount of money to be spent on pollution control.

Economists have long recognized the need for public regulation of economic activities that result in unwanted side effects. These effects — called "external diseconomies" in the language of economics — may arise whenever market forces alone are insufficient to make an individual bear all the costs resulting from his actions. Air pollution, which results from using air as a waste-disposal medium, is an excellent example of an external diseconomy, since there are clearly no market forces that compel the user to consider the costs he imposes on others. Without regulation, therefore, the air is used as if no such costs were present and air pollution rises to a level that is socially undesirable.

But despite their long-standing recognition of air pollution as a ubiquitous example of these side effects, economists have not undertaken studies that contribute significantly to answering the hard questions facing policy-makers. For example, what level of pollution is socially acceptable? What should be done to achieve this standard? How can costs be allocated fairly to all those who contribute to air pollution? What institutional arrangements will ensure effective use of the limited answers we have for these questions? Although such questions have been discussed increasingly in recent years, there has been no attempt to produce useful operational answers. For example, economists have recommended that an effluent charge or tax be levied on emissions in order to induce behavior that will lead to acceptable levels of air pollution. Of the various arguments made against this proposal, the most telling is that no one has ventured to suggest what the magnitude of such a charge should be or even how — except at an abstract level — to determine what it should be.

These operational questions have not been answered because they require empirical information far beyond our current understanding of the problem — information that will permit us to estimate the net social benefits (benefits minus costs) that would result from a given change in controls on emissions. But there are many causal links between controls and net benefits, and we need quantitative information about each link in order to specify the over-all relationship. We need to know how pollutors are likely to respond to given changes in controls, and the extent to which emission levels will be affected by changes in their activities (which include such ordinary and universal activities as producing goods, traveling, and disposing of trash). We need to know how a change in emission levels is likely to affect ambient air quality, a relationship that is strongly influenced by meteorological, topological, and climatic conditions. We need to know the relationship between ambient air quality and direct loss, a relationship obscured by the presence of many other, often more important, factors that cause the same type of losses. We need to know how individuals adjust to offset these losses. Finally, we need to measure the resulting losses in common terms so they can be added together and compared.

This list of requirements is not meant to suggest a council of perfection. Even crude approximations would permit some responsible judgments to be made. But the state of our knowledge is such that in many important cases even educated guesses about the specific form of these relationships are lacking.

In the face of these complex relationships, so inadequately understood and even less fully quantified, progress is most likely to be made by concentrating empirical efforts on fairly small links in the whole causal chain. . .

The difficulties in setting standards of ambient air quality are at the heart of most policy problems and raise all the measurement problems at issue in this study. Standard setting is therefore a useful context in which to present a frame of reference for describing the derived measurements.

Two lists would provide the raw material for a rational setting of air-pollution standards: in one, all the changes necessary to bring about a given alteration in air quality, and in the other all the consequences that result from this alteration. If the items in each list could be assigned realistic dollar values — and we will assume for the moment that this is possible — the lists would represent two broad categories of costs. The first will be called the "costs of control." Although the second is clearly a list of the "benefits of control," for the sake of a later discussion we will call it the "costs of pollution," since it represents the benefits foregone in the absence of controls. With rather grim humor, the first category could also be called the "benefits of pollution," for these are the costs that could be eliminated by permitting pollution to occur without regulation.

If costs for all the items in these lists can be estimated for each different level of pollution that is of interest for policy purposes, they could be conveniently represented as curves similar to those presented in Figure la. As the level of pollution rises above zero, the cost of pollution (curve *CP*) may remain at zero for a time, or appear to be zero because our measurements are not sensitive to the costs of very low pollution levels. But at some point *t,* the curve *CP* can be expected to begin rising and to continue rising at an increasing rate, eventually becoming vertical at extremely high concentrations where all life would cease. The cost of control (curve *CC*), on the other hand, is zero at point *r,* representing the level of pollution prevailing in the absence of controls. To reduce pollution below this point, costs must be increased. The *CC* curve eventually becomes vertical as it rises to the left, indicating that at those low levels of pollution all our resources cannot further reduce the concentration of the pollutant. For example, the elimination of all pollutants resulting from combustion is likely to require the elimination of all combustion; and because background radiation is always present, our exposure to radiation could not be entirely eliminated unless we lived in the equivalent of a lead box.

From a social point of view, the best level at which to set the standard is where both the costs of pollution and the costs of control, taken together, are minimum. Figures 1b and 1c are two different ways of showing this point of minimum cost. The curve shown in Figure 1b is the (vertical) sum of the *CP* and *CC* curves, the appropriate standard obviously indicated by point *s* where the curve reaches a minimum value. Figure 1c shows the marginal cost curves, each of which indicates how the corresponding curve in Figure 1a changes for a small change in the concentration of the pollutant.[1] Here, the appropriate standard is indicated by the point where the marginal cost of control (curve *MCC*) equals the marginal cost of pollution (curve *MCP*). Point *s* again represents that standard.[2] This equality indicates that, if we try to reduce the level of pollution by a small decrement, the cost of control would increase by an amount equal to the cost of the damage caused by the air pollution. Such a change is equivalent to moving a small distance within the trough of the (*CP* + *CC*) curve of Figure 1b. We gain nothing by inducing a change at that point; either an increase or a decrease in pollution from that level would entail an economic loss to society.

If measurements are to be useful within this analytical framework, they should possess certain characteristics. First, and most important,

Figure 1
Total costs, sum of total costs, and marginal costs

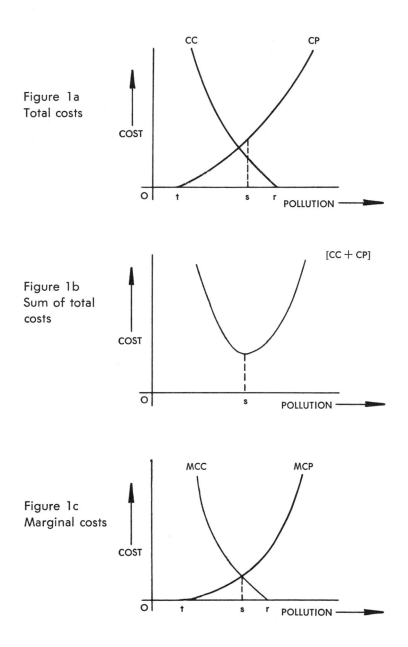

Figure 1a
Total costs

Figure 1b
Sum of total
costs

Figure 1c
Marginal costs

they must tell us more than the current *total* costs of pollution and of control; knowing only where we currently are on the curves of Figure 1a could be misleading. Informed decisions require a knowledge of the current *marginal* costs of pollution and of control, that is, where we are on the curves of Figure 1c. Marginal costs will at least indicate the direction in which, if not the exact point toward which, policy should move. In particular, the fact that the total costs of pollution are greater than the costs of control does not, by itself, indicate that optimal standards are being violated and that therefore more should be spent on control.

This point must be emphasized because all too often one reads statements implying the contrary. In an article in the *Saturday Review*, C.W. Griffin, Jr., relying on commonly quoted figures, stated:

> Even if air pollution presented no human health hazard whatsoever, we could justify a tremendous strengthening of control on purely economic grounds... The nation's total bill is estimated at $11 billion a year, about twenty times the most optimistic estimate of total national expenditures by industry and by all levels of government for control devices, research and enforcement programs.[3]

This statement is obviously based on the unstated (and unsupported) assumption that when there is such a large discrepancy between the cost of pollution and the cost of control (assuming for the moment that the estimates are reasonably correct), an additional million dollars spent on controls will reduce the costs of pollution by at least that much. This of course is conceivable, but it is also conceivable that an additional million will result in less than that amount of improvement. For example, considering only Figure 1a, at the level of pollution s corresponding to the standard set in Figures 1b and 1c, the total cost of pollution is higher than the total cost of control.[4] Following the argument implicit in the quoted paragraph, a community would spend money to move its pollution level to the left until the total costs were equal. But this would have moved the pollution level away from the point of minimum combined costs of pollution and control; that is, it would have increased the combined costs to that community. Empirical evidence on the marginal costs is therefore necessary to support any program of pollution control.[5]

The total cost of pollution at a given time may be useful for other reasons. Policy-makers may not give proposals a hearing, or even authorize an investigation unless they are first shown that the problem involved is a serious one, relative to others they must consider. For this purpose total cost is likely to be more impressive than the excess of marginal benefits over marginal costs; and figures such as those quoted above undoubtedly helped achieve the passage of the Clean Air Act of 1963. But once the proposal has obtained a hearing and the issue becomes what to do about the problem, the total cost figures are irrelevant.[6]

The second characteristic of useful measurements is that they should be made *within a specific air shed* and on *specific pollutants* (or groups of them if they act, or can be acted upon, together). Each pollutant has its own characteristics and each community faces different meteorological, topological, and economic conditions. The appropriate standard, therefore, will vary with the pollutant and the community being studied. This point suggests that national estimates of pollution and control costs are not useful for setting standards, even if they could be made in marginal terms. As a first approximation and a matter of convenience, we may wish to set some common standards for the nation as a whole; but even so, local rather than national data should be used for this purpose.

Third, the costs that are measured should be *minimum* costs. With respect to the costs of control, it is self-evident that the standard will not be set correctly unless each point on the curve represents the minimum cost of achieving the implied reduction in pollution levels. But the same is also true for costs of pollution. If it is cheaper for an asthma victim to move from an area than to continue suffering, only the losses he would incur in moving should be included in the cost of pollution curve. If this procedure is not followed, the standard could easily be set too low, considering the interests of the pollutor as well as those of the person who suffers from pollution.

This point has more relevance for research into the costs of control than it does for this study, for we have little choice but to assume that the observed costs of pollution damage are the minimum costs we wish to measure. In the case of the asthma victim who stays in the polluted area, we must assume that he knows what he is doing, i.e., that for him it is cheaper to stay than to move (perhaps because of the psychic costs involved in moving).[7] While this is equivalent to assuming rational and knowledgeable behavior, any other assumption would require us to look into the mind of each affected person to determine whether he is properly adjusting to the pollution damages he faces, a task far beyond the scope of this (and very likely any other) study. But cases can arise in which the assumption is clearly unjustifiable, and we must be prepared to adjust the cost estimates to make them useful for standard setting purposes.

Finally, point s will represent the appropriate standard only if the CC and CP curves do in fact measure and aggregate *all* the benefits and costs adequately. Actually, of course, many important consequences cannot be measured, and the policy-maker must use his intuition and judgment to modify the answer obtained from the quantitative analysis. To aid in this process a qualitative analysis of nonquantifiable variables should be included; at the very least such an analysis will indicate the direction of the biases imposed by the special assumptions and omissions involved in the quantitative studies.

It should be recognized that measurements with these characteristics ignore dynamic elements — the forces that tend to shift the CC and CP curves to the right or left. For example, the cost of pollution curve tends to shift to the right as activities giving rise to pollution and the number of objects subject to pollution damage grow over time, whereas the cost of control curve will shift to the left whenever a technological breakthrough in the control of pollution occurs. A change in tastes can also affect the shape or position of these curves. At a minimum, this additional dimension to the problem of standard setting requires that the cost curves be recalculated periodically to adjust the standard to new circumstances.[8]

In conclusion, it is useful to refer to the criticism that has been leveled against this analytical framework, namely, that so small a portion of the relevant consequences can be quantified that the effort is not worth it. Three points can be made in reply. First, the organization and structuring of the problem in terms that are useful for measurement and the clarification of issues that typically result may be much more useful to the policy-maker than the measurements themselves. Second, a consequence of this study should be a better understanding of the specific types of data needed to make future measurements more valuable. Third, and most important, this question cannot be settled *a priori*. There is no way to know in advance of measurement whether or not a usefully large portion of the consequences of a proposed action can be quantified. Of course, all relevant consequences of an action are unlikely ever to become measurable. But we can hope to whittle down the area within which unsupported opinion and emotive rhetoric dominate.

1 In other words, they are the first derivatives of the corresponding total curves with respect to a change in concentration of pollution except that, in order to present both curves in the same quadrant, the minus sign has been dropped from the *MCC* curve. Also to improve readability the scale has been changed.

2 Parenthetically, we might note that an effluent charge should in principal be set in such a way that the pollutor is faced with a scale of charges identical to the *MCP* curve. In this way he is forced to "internalize" the costs he forces others to bear and is induced to move to points.

3 C.W. Griffin, Jr., "America's Airborne Garbage," *Saturday Review*, May 22, 1965, p. 34.

4 This is purely a function of the position in which the curves have been drawn. Obviously curve *CP* could be shifted vertically – indeed, even shifted downward until *CP* is less than *CC* – without affecting the position of point *s* in Figure 1b or 1c.

5 In evaluating control programs that are expected to reduce the cost of a particular pollutant to zero, the total cost *is* the relevant marginal cost figure. The introduction of control equipment that will virtually eliminate the emission of fluorides from a specific plant is a case in point. But this is simply a special case of the general principle.

6 There are great, perhaps insurmountable, difficulties involved in estimating total costs. These are discussed in a 1966 report to the Division of Air Pollution entitled, *The Problem of Estimating Total Costs of Air Pollution, a Discussion and an Illustration*, by the present author. These difficulties raise further doubts about the value of the published estimates.

7 We must also assume that he does not stay in order to influence the determination of standards.

8 A more satisfactory procedure would be to set the standard after taking into account both the current and the expected future position of the cost and benefit schedules. A preliminary consideration of this problem and some estimates of the future air-pollution problem for one city can be found in *A Projection of Air Pollution Problems in St. Louis*, a 1966 report submitted by this author to the Division of Air Pollution, U.S. Public Health Service, and available from them.

On the Canada Water Act

The Canada Water Act, proposed by the federal government in 1969, is an important public document in the sense that it will establish the basis for future policy decisions about the quality of water in Canada. During the second reading of the bill in 1970, the Minister of Energy, Mines and Resources, the Honourable J.J. Greene, spoke of the need to act now in order to preserve Canada's water resources. The following is part of his speech which outlines the philosophy and economic reasoning behind the bill: water has many uses; waste disposal is not an illegitimate use of water; each water basin must be considered separately so that the maximum value can be obtained from the water's use, according to circumstances in the basin. The Act is reprinted here as Appendix 1.

Water is the medium in which life itself was spawned. It is the major constituent of the human body, an essential ingredient of the air we breathe, the principal feature of our weather, the habitat for myriad varieties of life forms and a major factor in all of man's undertakings.

It is, on the one hand, a source of awesome violence through deluge and flood and, on the other, an object of unparalleled natural beauty and the fount of spiritual rejuvenation for people of all ages.

For millions of years, man, like the more primitive animals before him, has lived along the shoreline of waterways. It is no accident that the great citadels of every civilization are almost without exception located in the vicinity of a major water body. But, as with so many of the bounties of nature, we have grown so accustomed to its presence that we fail to give it the attention and respect it deserves.

In time our indulgence, apathy, neglect and abuse have produced a resource that has sunk from being an object of beauty and utility to an unsightly and malodorous witness to the failure of man on his own planet. Far from being a source of inspiration, many of our rivers and lakes are the source of discontent and frustration and at times even a danger to our health and well being.

This is the situation with the once beautiful waterways that surround this very House. Debris, odour, dead fish, and high bacteria count are the normal summertime conditions surrounding many of the country's finest cities and even the very capital of this nation.

The time has come when every government, every industry, and every citizen must act in concert if we are to roll back pollution and thereafter manage our water resources for the optimum benefit of those who would use this precious heritage today and who will require it in our tomorrows . . .

At the beginning of the nineteenth century, when all of Canada was sparsely populated and none of her waters congested, there was water enough to drive logs, turn water-wheels and provide fish for our ancestors. But as I have mentioned already . . . our ancestors were then few, and the industries were indeed tiny. Waste, both human and industrial, was swallowed up by our rivers and quickly purified.

But as the population grew, villages expanded into cities and little saw mills became huge pulp and paper factories. However, our attitudes with respect to water and our practices did not change thereby. The new cities assumed that the nearby waterbody could still easily dispose of their waste, and they dumped in their leavings, in new abundance and untreated. Small industries, grown large, assumed that because a river could handle a few tons of sawdust and bark chips a day, it could as easily handle several hundred tons of wood fibres and sulphite effluent. More industries and more cities joined those already there. Hydro plants converted the fast flowing rapids, which rivers once used to cleanse themselves, into stagnant head-ponds, and each time another rapid was castrated bringing more hydro power, we cheered — and called it progress . . .

I believe we now realize that we have all erred. We have failed to plan the use of our waters. The time has surely come to pay the piper and redeem the wrong of yesterday.

For our flowing waters have many uses. Most of our rivers and lakes are used for recreation; for drinking water; for fishing; for irrigation; for hydro power generation, and yes, also for the disposal of waste. Not all of these uses can be reconciled easily. And yet they must be. This is our task. We do not question the use of streams for recreation or drinking or irrigation or hydro power or waste disposal. Yet each one of these uses may conflict with all of the other uses.

Seeing the pollution, many people now consider waste disposal to be an illegitimate use of water. But waste is an unavoidable factor of our modern way of life. Matter cannot be created or destroyed. Whatever we build, whatever we use, must somehow be disposed of, and disposal to most of us means getting our ugly discards out of our sight. We inevitably turn to water to transport this residue to the sea.

Waste disposal is not necessarily an illegitimate use for water and it does not necessarily interfere with other uses for water because our waterways, if not overloaded, can purify themselves. It is only when the natural ability of water to cleanse itself is surpassed that we find this use of water interfering with other uses of that precious resource.

All of this makes one point very clear. Our water must be so used as to ensure the maximum stream of benefits to all of the users for all of the purposes for which water is required. This optimization can only occur if we have comprehensive planning to achieve our goal of multi-purpose use. We must look at each basin as an integrated whole. We must examine all the uses which can be made of each basin. We must plan for the future so as to achieve the greatest long-term net social benefit of our water resources. The Canada water bill will allow us to do this – to plan together with the provinces firstly the optimum utilization of our water resources, taking into account all the uses which can be made of our water; and secondly, the re-establishment of water quality to preserve the best balance among these uses.

. . . we are facing a costly problem and we shall not avoid it. It will cost Canadian society some billions of dollars over a period of time to deal with its water resources in a rational way, and to undo the damage we have done in the last hundred years. But let us think of the alternate cost, that of doing nothing. To begin with, doing nothing is a threat to our entire way of life, and, yes, perhaps to life itself. Eventually, if we do not act to clean up air and water pollution, if we allow our environment to run down further we may upset the ecological and climatological balances of nature upon which life itself depends.

But even if the problem we face has not yet reached this peak, there are huge social costs involved. It is not hard to imagine the day – not far off if we do not act – when there will be no place within easy range of our cities where a person can go to swim in a natural river or lake, or any accessible place where fish can still live, or any place to just walk beside a pleasant stream. Our society will have its two cars in every garage but there will be no fit outdoor place to which to drive them. Yes, we will have our superclean, automatically washed clothes, but will there be any place fit to walk in these snow white garments? These are staggering social costs, costs that neither we nor our children will have to pay, if we act now.

Then, too, there are the purely monetary costs. Water despoiled by man must be cleaned again for his own use. The cost of purifying the water we have first made dirty is high. How much better to clean up our effluents before we put them into our rivers. For we then have the double benefit of clean water while it is in the stream, and drastically lowered purification costs when we want to use it again.

There are other monetary costs as well. The salmon run in certain maritime rivers may be dying because of our pollution. With it would die a source of revenue as well as of pleasure. Our other fisheries are also threatened by pollution, and with them would go the livelihood and the way of life of thousands of Canadians. Our tourist industry depends in no small part on the cleanliness of our streams, rivers and lakes . . . Without the use of our most important single resource, water, the future of the industry would be a bleak one indeed!

The problem has arisen from the unwise use of resources that come to us free of charge. The lesson which we can learn from the past is a vital one. It is simply this, that the unplanned and uncontrolled use of our resources, even though they come free, as does water, can lead us to disaster. The first principle of the Canada water bill, and of the thinking of experts of all persuasions across Canada, is that no longer can we afford the unplanned and uncontrolled use of our water resources. No longer can each individual, each industry, each municipality, use our water resources as each sees fit. In that absolute and laissez-faire freedom lies the mistake of the past, and the disaster of the future. Those who use our waters must pay for that use, either by cleaning up what they discharge into our river basins, or by paying others to clean it up for them. This is the very gist of the Canada Water Act and the essence of its structure, that the user must pay for cleaning the water, for putting it back into the condition in which he found it and for improving it if indeed it requires improvement. The result, it is true, may be higher direct costs for certain goods and services. But as we look at these costs, we must remember that there will be savings to other users of the water who also have a right to expect that the water they receive will be clean and in good condition when it reaches them. We must remember, too, that there is no way we can avoid these costs and still maintain the quality of life. Everyone in society must eventually pay; this is the thing we must remember, and all of society will thereby gain.

Physically or geographically, Canada represents in some ways a highly unique case in the problems of water resource management. We have a small population, yet we are endowed with huge river basins and enormous water resources. We have exploited these water resources one at a time to further our economic development. Our rivers have been transportation routes for our largest single industry, pulp and paper. They have provided the vast amounts of hydroelectric power necessary to operate the extractive industries which have helped to give us the standard of living we enjoy. Yes, in some ways our waters, and our rivers in particular, have been the very backbone of our economic development.

However, the magnitude of our water resources and the exceptionally heavy use we have made of them have produced problems of proportional magnitude. So, the first factor we must face is that of the enormity of the problem and the historical nature of the background which has led to it.

The second factor we must face is that, by its very nature, water admits of many uses. Not all, as I have said before, are compatible one with the other. This problem is compounded by the fact that our water resources are so large that a single river may be called upon to fulfil many uses in its journey to the sea. It may be used to transport logs, cool a thermal electric plant, generate hydroelectricity, provide water for cities, irrigate farm lands and carry industrial waste. Each of these different uses requires a different standard of quality and different controls of river flow volumes. Moreover, different river basins will have different mixes of these uses.

This suggested to us and to the planners the key principle that must be incorporated into the act. Obviously, the key principle is that of flexibility. This we tried to build into this legislation. We cannot impose the same formula on all waters in Canada, because our diverse waters have widely divergent uses and pass through widely different areas. It would, for example, be unreasonable and impractical to expect a busy harbour surrounded by a large city to attain the same degree of purity as a mountain trout stream. Its uses are vastly different. Society would be ill served by imposing the level of quality appropriate to Lake Louise on Hamilton Harbour. Nevertheless, because of their great volume, the effluents entering Hamilton Harbour will very likely require more treatment, and to a higher standard, than will the small volume of effluents entering Lake Louise. The Canada water bill, therefore, provides that we undertake comprehensive planning on a basin by basin basis.

. . . It is clear that the problems we are discussing are grave and urgent. Equally, the solutions we must produce are momentous in their scope. It is impossible to make an exact estimate of what it will cost us to pay for our past sins and establish a sound program for the future, but estimates range to billions of dollars.

Nor can we complete the job overnight. The damage it took us decades to do, will, even with our best efforts, take us years to undo. The 1970's in Canada will have to be dedicated to the eradication of pollution and the rational and comprehensive management of our resources.

Who will pay the gigantic costs involved? The answer to that is that just as everyone is responsible, so in the end everyone must pay.

Municipalities which deposit human and industrial waste in our waters must do their part. Here very special responsibilities for the clean-up and treatment of domestic and industrial sewage fall upon a level of government that is at the bottom of the fiscal totem pole and often finds itself in difficult financial straits. Through the provinces, which are responsible for the municipalities under our constitution, they will be consulted and must do their part. They must join the national effort, must plan for the future of their and our water resources. Yet we realize that the municipalities face a grave financial situation. Consequently, we are taking steps through Central Mortgage and Housing Corporation to make a large and expanding fund available from which municipalities may borrow under favourable circumstances in order to finance the construction of sewage treatment facilities. The present shortage of loan funds, which some have pointed to as a result of the present financial difficulties and the determination of the government to fight the war on inflation, is temporary and will be rectified.

And what of the individual citizen? What does he contribute to this program and to his challenge of the times? First, we must remember that it is he who makes up the totality of our body politic, and so the quality of our environment must depend ultimately upon him. Each of us has exploited our environment for too long and the cost has become evident. Dying lakes and rivers surround us and the smell of pollution is everywhere. The cost of phosphate-filled detergents is algae choked lakes. The cost of the sixty-page coloured advertising supplement in our daily paper is sulphite liquor and wood fibres in once clean rivers. The eventual cost of our way of life may be its extinction unless the individual citizen is willing to pay the price of cleaning up our environment. It is ultimately a matter of the attitude of the private citizen that will control the whole success of this venture. Public opinion must remain strong on this issue. We must all demand that the job be done and the price be paid if we are to win the struggle.

Having spoken of the responsibility of municipalities and of the individual himself in this struggle, may I now concern myself with industry, so often a whipping boy when we talk of questions of pollution. How often in recent months have I seen the ire of citizens directed at polluters in everything from letters to the editors, to the learned articles and academic publications, and inevitably industry is the villain, industry is the sinner and industry must pay, then all our troubles will be over. How easy and happy the solution would be. Yes, industry must pay its burden of the costs. We must recall that industry in fact is all of us as employers, employees and consumers of industrial products. It is all of us as recipients of the vast sum and taxes paid by industry.

Millions of Canadians work in industry and hundreds of thousands, at least, are owners of industry within the framework of the capitalistic system. Each and every one of us consume the products of industry. To indict industry as the sole culprit, is little more than indicting ourselves, as industry does little more or less than public opinion demands. More than this, industry has surely not behaved much differently than have we, as individual citizens.

Yes, industry is bigger and will have to be cleaner, and accordingly its clean-up costs will be greater than that of individuals. This is not to defend industry but rather to point out that the corporate citizen has done little different but is only bigger than the individual citizen and must bear the cost in proportion.

Yes, industry must in fact indicate its willingness to co-operate in this great effort to improve the quality of our environment. The private enterprise system, with its inherent freedom, giving the maximum choice to the individual, rewarding initiative and industry — that very freedom and incentive which the capitalistic system has given — has provided a real reward in the highest standard of living that any system known to man up to the time of this system has given.

The system unquestionably has faults. There are those who claim the private enterprise system has lost its sense of purpose and morality. Hence, to some degree the disaffection of youth who refuse to subscribe to its purposes, and the unrest on the street and on the campus. Dissenters from Eugene Debs to the current disciple of dissent, Paul Goodman, have railed at its deficiencies; but perhaps Galbraith has put dissent in more useful terms in pointing to the deficiencies by refusing to tear down the house merely that we might repair the plumbing. He has, as I understand it, suggested reform rather than demolition. He has urged that the great corporations of the private sector who play a paramount part in the direction and purposes of our economy and society must devote a far greater proportion of their leadership, drive and productivity to the public sector as well as to private profit and the benefits to be derived from insiders of the system if the system is to survive in the tomorrows.

This surely is the great test of our times. Those of us who believe in the freedom and the individuality and the productivity of that system know full well that it must divert some of the great energies and production it unleashes to the quality of our life and our environment, as well as to the corporate profit motivation and to the financial well-being of its own. If it does not do so, the alternative will clearly be a greater control by government, more state-ism, and possibly an ultimate state control of the instruments of production which has nowhere, to my knowledge, proved either conducive to freedom or productivity. But if the system fails in these measures and in these directions to play a more useful part in the public sector then it will pass from the scene of history as did the systems of Egypt, the Byzantine empire, Rome or Greece when they failed to serve the people they purported to serve.

It may well be that in Canada we do have decay in our purposes and in our spirit, with our high standard of living, in respect of things as important as protecting our environment and our water. But I do believe we in Canada have the will to act, and to act in time, if our spirits have decayed and if we have permitted the despoliation of our waters. I believe the will exists and, in fact, that the Canadian people demand that we act and act now to restore and preserve our waters and the quality of our environment.

We are no longer willing to sacrifice the health and beauty of our surroundings on the altar of economic growth or so-called standard of living which serves self but takes little care of the environment and replacing things for those who come after. Here in Canada we have continued for so long to search for that elusive Canadian identity. May I have the temerity to suggest that no identifying characteristic of Canadians would be more worthy than our observable commitment to a recognizable Canadian ethic which proclaimed that henceforth we will include the quality of our environment in our calculus of progress . . .

Environmental pollution

The expenditure, be it private or public, to control waste disposal and restore water and air will occupy an increasing share of gross national product in the nineteen seventies. The Economic Council of Canada referred to environmental pollution in its Sixth Annual Report, *Perspective 1975*, identifying sources of air and water pollution in Canada. Their remarks are included in the following selection. Because of the potentially large sums of money involved and the impact of this on the private and public sector, one would hope that the Council will devote considerably more time and energy to this problem in the near future.

The Council recognizes that environmental pollution is far too complex a problem — with a wide variety of technical, economic and social aspects — to be dealt with adequately in a few pages. What follows is merely a preliminary attempt to sketch the dimensions of two of our pollution problems — air and water pollution — as a beginning towards the setting of objectives in this troublesome area. In our future work, we intend to undertake a more extensive and systematic analysis of these and other pollution problems.

Although we recognize that some significant efforts and contributions are already being made to pollution abatement by various governments and business firms, examples of serious environmental pollution in Canada are not difficult to document. Moreover, not only are there some serious problems now; in the absence of additional effective abatement programs, they will tend to intensify in the future with increasing population, urbanization and industrial output. Yet in reaching for constructive solutions it will be important to avoid the temptation merely to play up the dramatic impact of these problems, and to begin to analyse them in an increasingly comprehensive framework that will cover the environment as a whole and allow for a variety of approaches including both public and private expenditures, incentives and regulations.

This framework must recognize the complex technical relationships among the various forms of pollution. It must also recognize the complex economic and social nature of the problems. Pollution entails costs — frequently costs to society that are not readily apparent. On the other hand, it is also important to recognize that pollution abatement also entails costs — here, too, costs that may not be readily apparent. It will therefore be important to set out reasonable objectives of pollution abatement, having careful regard to a balance of both the costs and benefits of such abatement within the larger framework of social and economic goals.

WATER POLLUTION

The consequences of water pollution include inadequate water supplies, the menace of health, destruction of fish and other aquatic life, loss of recreation areas and the creation of a generally disagreeable environment. The primary sources of such pollution are domestic and industrial wastes.

The effects of inadequate facilities for disposal of these wastes are not confined to a few large urban areas or to a few regions of the country. Table 1 indicates the widespread nature of the problem. It should be emphasized, however, that the intensity of the problem differs substantially from place to place, and at different times and under different conditions.

TABLE 1
Selected Water Basins Significantly Affected by Pollution

REGION	WATER BASIN
Atlantic Region	Saint Croix River Basin
	Annapolis River Basin
	Saint John River Basin
	Miramichi River Basin
Eastern Ontario and Quebec	Rideau River Basin
	Ottawa River Basin
	St. Lawrence River Basin
	Upper Yamaska Watershed
Great Lakes Region	Maitland River Basin
	Don River Basin
	Lake Erie
	Lake Ontario
Prairie Region and Western Ontario	Rainy River Basin
	North Saskatchewan River Basin
	Bow and South Saskatchewan River Basin
	Red River Basin
British Columbia	Fraser River Basin

NOTE: Various water uses, such as fisheries and spawning grounds, recreational activities, aquatic life and industrial water supplies, are impaired or threatened collectively in at least some parts of the above water basins, although each water basin has its own particular problems and these vary also within each basin.
SOURCE: Based on data from Departments of Energy, Mines and Resources; Fisheries and Forestry; and National Health and Welfare.

This table does not pretend to be comprehensive; it is merely illustrative, and could also have included rivers such as the Grand and the Thames in Southern Ontario where, at certain points, bacterial counts have at times been as high as in raw domestic sewage. Similarly, in the other regions of the country, there are a multitude of examples of water pollution, particularly in the vicinity of high population density and of substantial industrial activity.

Industries and even single firms contribute to the level of pollution in remote as well as heavily populated areas; indeed the polluting

TABLE 2
Sewage treatment in selected urban areas, 1969

Metropolitan Area	Wastewater Flow	Percentage of Wastewater Flow Subject to:		
		No Treatment	Primary	Secondary
	(Million gallons per day)			
St. John's	12.7	100.0		
Halifax-Dartmouth	9.9	99.0	1.0	
Saint John	5.4	99.8		0.2*
Quebec	42.0	100.0		
Montreal	290.2	91.6	2.6	5.8
Ottawa	40.0		100.0	
Toronto	194.0			100.0
Hamilton	60.0		100.0	
Sudbury	11.0			100.0*
London	28.0			100.0
Windsor	4.0	85.0	**	15.0
Winnipeg	46.3	4.0		96.0*
Regina	12.0			100.0*
Saskatoon	10.0	93.0		7.0*
Edmonton	37.5		46.5	53.5*
Calgary	38.8		100.0	***
Vancouver	100.0	59.0	41.0	
Victoria	18.0	98.9		1.1

NOTE: Primary treatment removes 30-50 per cent of nonsuspended solids; secondary treatment removes about 80-85 per cent of total solids and reduces the biological oxygen demand by about the same proportion.

* Part or all of the treatment is in lagoons, which can be regarded as close to secondary treatment.

** Primary treatment plant to be completed in late summer 1969.

*** Secondary treatment facilities being constructed.

SOURCE: Based on data from Department of National Health and Welfare and the Metropolitan Corporation of Greater Winnipeg.

effluents of saw-mills, pulp and paper mills, mining firms and agricultural product processing plants frequently arouse more comment because their isolation singles them out for attention. Efforts to control harmful plants and insects that destroy forests and crops, to improve agricultural yields by fertilizing land, and to reduce winter driving hazards by salting streets and highways, also contribute to the pollution of rivers and lakes.

Many municipalities have little or no sewage treatment capacity and simply dump raw sewage. Moreover, in many other municipalities that have sewage treatment facilities, these do not appear to be adequate for the rising demands placed on them. Table 2 illustrates the very uneven pattern of sewage treatment capabilities in leading Canadian metropolitan areas.[1]

The fact that these problems exist now is worrisome. But water consumption tends to rise more rapidly than population. Moreover, rising demands of both households and industries have usually been accompanied by the emergence of more complex pollutants, such as detergents and other synthetic chemicals. Consequently, the existing problems can be expected to intensify unless present programs for abatement are further accelerated.

AIR POLLUTION

Less information is available on air than water pollution. Available information, sparse as it is, suggests that some of the major air pollutants exist at damaging levels in parts of Canada at certain periods.

The Air Pollution Control Service in Ontario has indicated that air pollution problems occur in most of that province's industrialized cities as shown in Chart 1. Unfortunately, similar data do not appear to be publicly available for cities in other provinces, with a few exceptions such as Vancouver.

It has been estimated that roughly 60 per cent of urban air pollution can be traced to the automobile. In Montreal, during the transit strike of October 1967, health department tests showed downtown peaks of carbon monoxide concentrate approaching dangerous levels.

Evidence suggests that damage to certain crops in Southern Ontario in recent years — notably white beans and tobacco — is due to

pollutants from Detroit, Windsor, Sarnia, Cleveland, Toledo and
Pittsburgh and other distant centres.

Chart 1
A measure of air pollution
over selected Ontario cities
1968

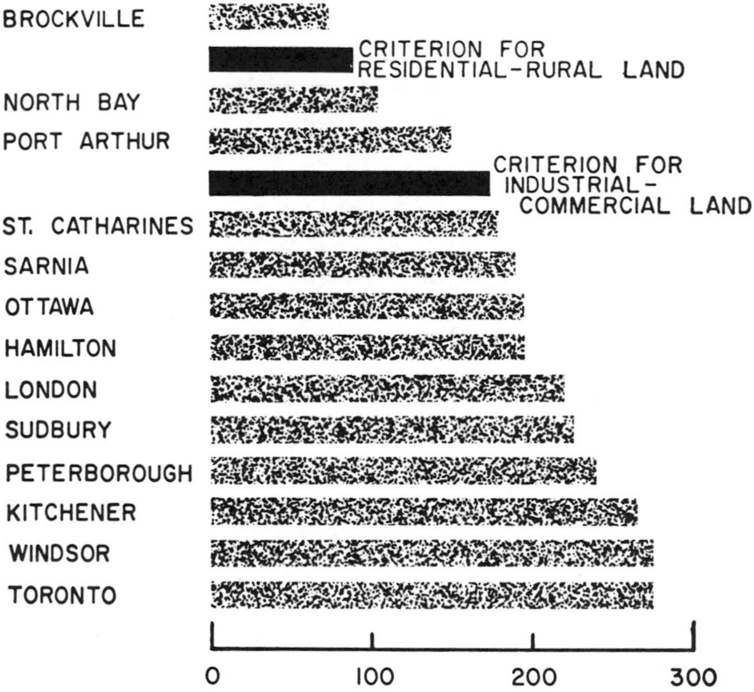

BROCKVILLE	
	CRITERION FOR RESIDENTIAL–RURAL LAND
NORTH BAY	
PORT ARTHUR	
	CRITERION FOR INDUSTRIAL–COMMERCIAL LAND
ST. CATHARINES	
SARNIA	
OTTAWA	
HAMILTON	
LONDON	
SUDBURY	
PETERBOROUGH	
KITCHENER	
WINDSOR	
TORONTO	

0   100   200   300

Note: This Chart depicts comparable measures of suspended particulate
matter which is only one of several possible measures of air pollution. Suspended
particulates comprise small air-borne particles of solids and low-volatility liquids.
These readings represent conditions at specific locations, not over the entire city
at all times. Air samples are taken over 24-hour periods at various times throughout the year. The criteria shown are set by the Ontario Air Pollution Control
Service. For example, to meet the criterion for industrial-commercial land, 90
per cent of the samples should be below a level of 175 micrograms per cubic
metre of air.
    Source: Based on data from Ontario Department of Health.

In attempts to deal more effectively in the future with pollution problems, several points must be borne in mind. Many pollution problems, perhaps particularly air pollution, cross jurisdictional boundaries. Moreover, the various forms of pollution are highly interdependent. What goes into our system of production and consumption must, apart from recycling or addition to inventories, come out as waste in some form. Any reduction in some form of waste discharge is normally accompanied by an increase in another kind — incineration of municipal and industrial refuse, for example, can easily lead to air pollution. Effective measures for dealing with pollution problems can therefore develop only within a framework that achieves adequate and consistent co-ordination among all jurisdictions involved and that has careful regard to the complex interrelationships between the various forms of pollution.

The sparsity of the information available shows the urgent need for greater research effort and inspection programs. Our estimates for government expenditures make allowance for stepped-up efforts to deal more adequately with these problems. But increased private efforts will also be needed. We believe that it is vitally important to move in this direction to maintain the quality of the human environment, and it is important that we proceed to build up efforts in this field over the next few years to avert the possible development of major "pollution crises" at some future time.

Part 3

Economic and financial aspects of pollution abatement

Economic decisions about pollution control

At the Pollution and our Environment Conference held in Montreal in 1966, Professors A.D. Scott and J.F. Graham presented a paper which discussed, in broad terms, some of the important economic factors to be considered in decision-making about pollution control. In their presentation, which follows, the authors emphasize the value of using a benefit-cost framework to aid in decision-making, while stressing some of the difficulties involved in attempting to quantify benefits and costs.

PART I   INTRODUCTION

Discussions of pollution and its control or elimination are frequently long on emotive presumption and short on analysis. There is a common tendency on the part of the conservationist and the layman to say pollution is harmful and wasteful — that it is obviously a bad thing — and that therefore it must be eliminated. In the face of the despoliation of our environment this is a plausible position. What other rational response can there be to the mounting evidence that our rivers are being turned into sewers, our city air charged with noxious fumes and our soil contaminated? Yet, however sympathetic the economist may personally be with this view, he cannot, as an economist, make offhand judgments about the desirability of pollution control. It is his professional responsibility to consider the expected costs of pollution control or elimination and to set these against the anticipated benefits. He must ask whether benefits will exceed costs or at what point costs of additional pollution abatement will exceed benefits. He must also ask who is to pay the costs and why. There are no simple answers either theoretically or empirically. Benefits to some may be obtained at a cost to others, and benefits and costs may be distributed unevenly. Benefits and costs may be difficult to determine and to measure.

It is the purpose of this paper to consider the economic basis for reaching decisions about pollution control. The approach of weighing benefits from any public project against its costs in deciding whether or not to undertake it is called "benefit-cost analysis". It is useful to explore the application of this technique to pollution control.

The need for benefit-cost analysis arises in deciding whether to produce a public good and how much of it because there is no market mechanism that enables each individual to determine how much of each public good he will purchase, as there is in the private economy. Public goods are generally indivisible. An individual cannot determine how much or what kind of national defence, public education, or pollution control is to be at his disposal. The amount provided depends upon a collective decision, as does the apportionment of the cost. Of course, even in the private economy the equating of costs and benefits is predicated on some given income distribution, which cannot be assumed to be sacrosanct.

Part of this paper is concerned with explaining the nature of benefit-cost analysis and is intended mainly to provide the context for questions explored in Part III, which constitutes the body of the paper. Part III considers the problems of distribution, i.e., the analytical difficulties that arise from the benefits of pollution control accruing to different people in different circumstances than those who bear the costs. The distributional question arises both within a single jurisdiction and between different jurisdictions and is likely to give rise to greater difficulties in a federal country with divided sovereignty than in a unitary state. It is hoped that this discussion will help to illuminate some central issues in the formulation of pollution-control policy.

This paper is not intended to be a blueprint for benefit-cost analysis or a detailed explanation of it. Rather, it is intended to consider the role of benefit-cost analysis in economic decision-making in the context of this particular conference.

PART II   A BRIEF DESCRIPTION OF BENEFIT-COST ANALYSIS AS APPLIED TO POLLUTION CONTROL

Benefit-cost analysis is simply the term used for systematic assessment of the direct and indirect, tangible and intangible, benefits and costs of a project or a number of alternative proposals for projects, so that in the case of a given proposal it can be determined if it is economically feasible, i.e., if benefits outweigh costs and, in the case of a number of alternative proposals, which among them yields the highest benefits in relation to costs (benefit-cost ratio). Economic feasibility presupposes technical feasibility; an investigation of the technical aspects of a proposal must therefore precede benefit-cost analysis.

Direct benefits are gains to those who use the good being provided — swimming in unpolluted water; indirect benefits are ones which are induced by the project — a bathing-suit factory; intangible benefits are ones which cannot usually be bought or sold at a price. Swimming would be a direct intangible benefit. The bathing-suit factory would gather indirect tangible benefits.

Direct costs are the value of the goods and services required to construct and operate a project — purification of the water; indirect costs are those incurred in the production of secondary benefits — the goods and services required to produce the bathing suits; intangible costs are ones not determined in the market.

The final decision as to whether or not to proceed with a given project is not determined simply by the expectation that it will yield greater benefits than costs, i.e., have a benefit-cost ratio greater than one, but by how its benefit-cost ratio compares with the ratio of other comparable expenditures.

In the case of private projects (and some governmental projects), they must not only have a benefit-cost ratio greater than one but must be financially self-sufficient. The essence of the typical public project, on the other hand, is that it is not financially self-sufficient because of the intangibility and/or indivisibility of its flow of benefits.

Basically, pollution is the impairment of the quality of water, soil, or air, so that the enjoyment of subsequent use by others is reduced and prevented. In the case of pollution abatement, the measurement of benefits is made difficult by their intangible nature. The easiest kind of benefits to estimate are those measured by costs saved, such as those saved by downstream users who previously had to purify water. Less easy to estimate are increases in regional net income owing to purer water and soil and the greater attractiveness of an unpolluted environment for the generation of new industry, bringing new jobs and new incomes. The difficulty here is that of predicting the effect of such an environment on this generation and of weighing it against other determinants of industrial location. Even more difficult is the problem of detecting and measuring the intangible benefits of pollution abatement, stemming from the indivisibility of its benefits. Its value is not determined in the market as is the case of private goods.

Nevertheless, it is possible to make at least rough estimates of some of the benefits and to list others to compare with the costs of a pollution abatement project. Such costs would be measured in terms of the new expenditures that must be made, production foregone, and increased production expenses. In the case of water pollution, purification costs can be estimated for existing and anticipated effluents. If the project induces emigration of waste-producing industries and activities, the foregone incomes may have to be taken into account, depending upon the size of jurisdiction. Such emigration will be a loss to the locality in question but not necessarily to a province, a region, or the nation. Where a choice presents itself, such as treatment of water pollution at its source or downstream, then of course the analysis must be applied to the alternatives, for the benefits and costs will likely be different for each of them.

The major problem of distribution, the main focus of this paper, is taken up in Part III. The findings in that part indicate that there are inherent limitations in the use of benefit-cost analysis for pollution abatement projects and, for that matter, for public goods in general. This is not to deny that benefit-cost analysis is pertinent and helpful, but rather to say that it is not always sufficient in itself for economic decision-making.

Probably the main contribution of benefit-cost analysis is not that it merely helps to determine whether to purify wastes, but that it helps to determine what degree of purification should be provided and the extent to which the cost should be privately and publicly borne. There are three ways in which it has a bearing on economic decision-making. Any program is subject to budgetary restraint. Benefit-cost analysis helps to determine the optimum budget for the public contribution to pollution abatement both absolutely and in relation to the competing claims of other programs and to ensure the best use of that budget. There are also the restraints imposed by the amounts of resources themselves. By assessing benefits and costs of pollution abatement in water, air, and soil, the analysis helps to determine the best use of these scarce resources. Finally, by considering the benefits and costs of alternative means of abatement, the cheapest means of achieving it can be found.

There are, of course, important technical details to consider in the course of such analysis. In evaluating a project and in making comparisons with other projects, it is necessary to express anticipated future costs and benefits in terms of present values by discounting the value of future costs and benefits at the appropriate rates, taking risk with respect to future costs and benefits into account. A small public authority should use the rate at which it can borrow or the yield on its investments for discounting benefits and costs. A senior government or its agency should use the typical yield for the national economy, from public and private use of funds, i.e., an estimate of the opportunity cost of funds that would be used in the pollution abatement project, for discounting both benefits and costs, since the discounting of costs and of benefits has the same significance in forms of opportunities foregone. Predictable risks can be allowed for in estimating costs. Allowance for unpredictable risks can probably best be made by using conservative estimates of uncertain benefits and costs, rather than by adding a risk component to the discount rate.

It is apparent that the analysis will be affected by the point of view, i.e., the size of jurisdiction being considered — city, metropolitan area, county, province, nation. What is a cost to a small locality, as in the case of a firm emigrating as a result of a pollution abatement program that imposes some or all of the costs upon it, will not be a net cost to the nation if the firm remains within national boundaries. Moreover, there may be benefits outside the locality, in addition to those accruing within it, as in the case of downstream users of purified water. In the case of pollution abatement, it is likely that the benefits will be greater (through "spillovers"), and the net costs less, the larger the jurisdiction being considered. On the other hand, a project considered from the national point of view may neglect the regional incidence of benefit and costs, i.e., it may have a favourable benefit-cost ratio nationally but an unfavourable one in some regions. The size of the jurisdiction for a project is generally determined by political rather than economic considerations. The problem is similar to the question of whether the focus should be on national economic development, i.e., on getting the largest total output from the nation's resources, or whether there should be some modification of this goal in the "interest" of regional development. The extent to which the national focus is acceptable to the lagging regions depends on the nature and extent of redistribution of income through federal-provincial and provincial-municipal fiscal transfers.[1]

The object of the benefit-cost analysis is ideally to provide the basis, in terms of net benefits and benefit-cost ratios, for a decision whether or not to proceed with a project or which of a number of alternative projects is to be preferred. While such analysis should be exploited as far as it is useful, the next and main part of this paper discusses some of the difficulties of applying it to pollution abatement and, at the same time, suggests other ways of looking at the decision-making process.

PART III DISTRIBUTIONAL CONSIDERATIONS
IN DECISION-MAKING

The previous part showed why benefit-cost analysis is sometimes recommended for analysing pollution problems and discussed the practical problems in its use. Being little more than an outline of the study of the problem by the application of the more widely accepted portions of "welfare economics," its further extension can go in one of two ways. The discussion may move "down" to the difficult details of actual analyses; or "up" to determine in what ways the motions and abstractions of welfare economics can provide guidance for policy action. In the following paragraphs the "up" route is followed.

In this part we deal, then, with three circumstances which may cause economists to hesitate to take seriously the results of a benefit-cost analysis of a pollution situation which has been correctly undertaken in detail. In the jargon of economics, these three circumstances are described as "distributional," since they relate to the distribution of costs or benefits among persons in differing circumstances. If all persons were identical (in income, family size, tastes, needs, location, and so forth) there would be no need to take account of the distribution of costs and benefits for, by assumption, what was a cost or benefit to one would affect all the others to the same extent. Then the total costs or benefits to an entire region would be a simple multiplication of those accruing to a typical person.

But in the situations where it is proposed to do something about pollution, the effects of the proposed action do not affect everyone equally. Circumstances are such that, before the anti-pollution action is taken, people differ in their incomes, their location (i.e., the jurisdiction in which they live and pay taxes), and their tastes. We deal with the analytical consequences of these three circumstances in turn.

It must be admitted that similar distributional circumstances may invalidate a benefit-cost analysis of any problem. Pollution is not unique. However the fact that the sufferers from pollution may be far from its source and the fact that the suffering of pollution and the enjoyment of its removal must be collectively experienced by a large number of persons, both suggest that distributional considerations may be more important in the benefit-cost analysis of pollution problems than of some other objects of this procedure.

A.   The distribution of income

This section deals with the most common and pervasive weakness of benefit-cost analysis in any application: that income is not evenly distributed among persons who bear the costs or enjoy the benefits of pollution control. Indeed, in many public-works projects, of which pollution control is merely a case, nothing is equally divided; some people pay all the costs and another group of people get all the benefits. But in this section we assume that the costs are spread widely over the same group of people who get the benefits, so as to simplify the confrontation of the differences-in-income problem.

Benefit-cost analysis tries to overcome the lack of a market situation in making large-scale investment decisions. If there were a market, commercial firms could discover how much people are willing to pay for a service, how much it would cost to supply such services, and whether there was a profit to be made from going into that business, although even here social costs in excess of private costs and social benefits in excess of private benefits have to be taken into account in evaluating the social performance of market-regulated production. Indeed, the commonest examples of social costs exceeding private costs are air and water pollution. But there is usually no market for the benefits of pollution control, either because the good is a public good, or because it is inconvenient, costly, or contrary to public policy to charge for the service in question. In such circumstances, good benefit-cost procedure calls for a "simulation" of the market, to discover what people would be willing to pay even though they will never be asked directly to pay a price, fee or toll. In the most difficult cases, as in air pollution reduction, this task amounts to little more than intelligent guesswork. But usually it is possible to discover how much people and firms would gain in incomes and profits if the service were provided, and so to work back to find how much they ought to be willing to pay, as a maximum. It can be shown that such calculations amount to learning how much revenue an industry producing the good (benefit from pollution control) would earn if it could operate in a competitive market.

The problem created by the unequal distribution of income arises when benefit-cost analysis is being used to compare alternative ways of dealing with pollution. We can make the point in discussing either benefits or costs.

Assume that two projects have identical costs, borne by the same persons. And assume that analysts have estimated that the two sets of benefits have identical totals. Both have been estimated by ascertaining what beneficiaries are actually willing to pay to enjoy the project. The first project's benefits accrue entirely to rich people, so that the amounts they would have to pay to enjoy it are small amounts of their annual incomes. The second project's benefits, on the other hand, accrue entirely to very poor people, so that the amounts they are willing to pay represent, for them, diversions of spending from food, clothing, and shelter.

Most people (and most economists) would say that the fact that the two groups are willing to contribute equal amounts for the projects should not be interpreted to mean that the projects have "equal value." The "utility" of the second project must be the higher, because poor people are anxious to give up large proportions of their small incomes to get it. Their dollar-ballots are usually (and rightly in our opinion) assumed to be more high-powered indicators of usefulness or necessity than the dollar-ballots of rich people.

But benefit-cost analysis cannot distinguish between the two projects' benefits to take account of the unequal distribution of income. (Nor can it, of course, take account of the fact that society may want to give a higher weight to the dollar-ballots of certain groups even if they are not poor, but are thought to be worthy for some other reason.) In the benefit-cost procedure, a dollar is a dollar, to whomsoever the benefit may accrue. This lack of sensitivity to the way income distribution affects the calculation of benefits may be a serious defect in accepting the procedure's findings.

Similarly, two alternative projects having identical physical benefits may have equal dollar costs that must however be borne in different ways. The first project will be paid for out of the income taxes of wealthy men. The second will be financed out of the sales taxes of widows and orphans buying bread and beer. Have the two projects equal worth? Most economists would agree with laymen in saying "no," the second project has the higher cost in the sense of imposing "a greater burden on society."

Economics has no way of verifying that, to society, a dollar of extra income or cost is more significant to poor people than to rich. But most economists surely reflect their own societies in claiming that it is. If they are correct, then the results of benefit-cost analysis in the comparison of alternatives must be accepted only sceptically, or else further analysis must be undertaken.

The further analysis may deal with either of two questions. (a) The analyst may attempt to discover whether the two alternatives do differ in the way they impinge on people of differing incomes. This is the easiest route to follow, because if the answer is in the negative, the original finding of the analysis may be accepted. (b) But if it is believed or found that the results of the analysis would be different if the distributions of income were different, then the analyst must wrestle, for each project, with the following questions: Is there some way of simultaneously redistributing income so that the project does not fall undesirably on poor people? Is the new distribution of income socially preferable to that ruling before the project was introduced ? And which of the two projects brings about a better redistribution of income?

Obviously, these are very difficult problems for analysis. But they occur continually in benefit-cost calculations on all subjects. They are certainly not confined to analysis of pollution problems, but because of the widespread diffusion of pollution-control benefits and the particular ways suggested for paying for these benefits (e.g., their being paid for by taxes, by industry, or by government as a grant) they are certainly more important here than in other applications.

B.   The distribution of jurisdiction

This section deals with an aspect of pollution-control projects that is not always encountered in other types of public-works projects. We refer to the fact that the source of pollution is often found in one community (jurisdiction), while the chief sufferers are located elsewhere. Benefit-cost analysis may show that the sufferers' losses are far greater than the costs of preventing the pollution. But now the problem is that entirely different groups of persons are affected.

For example, assume that the pollution of a river can only be dealt with at its source in an upstream community, while the only beneficiaries live many miles downstream. Assume that the two communities have equal sizes, incomes, and tastes. Of what significance now would be a benefit-cost finding that those downstream would value the removal of the pollution at more dollars than the upstream cost of removal? At best it would amount to a prediction that, if the two jurisdictions were allowed to bargain with one another about a contract for removing the source of pollution, an agreement advantageous to both parties would actually be reached.

Indeed, an agreement between neighbours about the "spillovers" from their domestic activities is one of the best ways to solve the problems of limited jurisdictions. This solution requires merely that jurisdictions of similarly-minded people exist and that each has power to negotiate with its neighbours. Then a sort of "market" in pollution-removal has been created, and benefit-cost analysis is replaced by actual bargaining.

When neighbouring jurisdictions, however, are each a conglomerate of different kinds of persons, it may be that local governments can hardly think of themselves as representative of a party to a bargain with a single aim. In reality, local governments govern both employers that produce pollution and hospitals that deal with victims of pollution, and yet they are directly involved in operating municipal sewage and waterworks plants. In such a confused situation, they are unlikely to take the role of buyer or seller in bargaining with neighbours, at least not for years after they have begun to study the matter.

Political theorists and economists interested in public finance have suggested ways that government structures could be adapted to deal with such complex situations.

(a) An inter-jurisdiction special-purpose authority may be created which, in the case of water pollution and water use, should presumably be coterminous with a watershed or discrete basin thereof. It can then look at the problem from one of two points of view: (i) as though it were a senior government (this is discussed below); (ii) as though it were a commercial venture unrestricted by boundaries, which can buy and sell services to all the jurisdictions it represents. This is the form in which waterboards and harbour authorities are frequently set up. But would it work in the case of pollution? We doubt it. For it would not have the legal or moral authority to impose costs on one area in order to clean up the environment in another. Neither would it have the finances to work on behalf of the sufferers.

(b) A senior level of government can take over the entire problem. Conducting a benefit-cost analysis, it can decide that pollution should be stopped (and proceed to enforce an ordinance, compensate those who have to install expensive control facilities, tax those who pollute to compensate those who suffer, or otherwise deal with the situation).

   This change in structure amounts to adopting a wider "point of view" and to ignoring the differences in the circumstances of the two separate communities. It is thus vulnerable to criticisms similar to those raised against the disregard of income differences. In effect, it amounts to sweeping the spillover question under the carpet. United States' benefit-cost procedures require that analyses be conducted from a national point of view — that is, that geographical differences in circumstances be ignored. This results from a political view of econ-omic society which is perhaps less acceptable in Canada. However, to the extent that the political structure of the country is designed essentially to give the nation, provinces, and localities control over matters respectively of national, provincial, and local concern, choos-ing the wider point of view — it may be provincial or national — has much to commend it in political logic.

   This political view, moreover, has one strong possible economic underpinning. Looking at inter-regional differences from a national point of view can be justified if it is felt that people and capital are highly mobile among regions. If they are, then the "national point of view" often amounts to making the best use of resources and locations with the knowledge that injured persons will take themselves and their property to other regions where they are none the worse off.

   There is a great deal to recommend this version of a national point of view. We have considered the potentialities of mobility among and within regions as a means of increasing the average and marginal productivity of labour throughout the entire nation.[2] But it must be admitted that to make decisions about water pollution control an instrument of factor mobility among regions is to go a good deal further than national opinion in Canada today appears to find acceptable. It is likely, however, that the larger the jurisdiction over which the pollution control measures are applied, the less is the opportunity for a person or a business firm to escape from costs (avoid injury) and the less pertinent therefore is the question of mobility.

   Finally, a senior government may use benefit-cost procedures to analyse the advisability of its acting as an intermediary between the two jurisdictions. For example, it might tax the upstream community in order to compensate the downstream community for its loss of amenity. Conversely, it might tax the downstream community to compensate the upstream community for the expense of preventing the pollution. By way of compromise between these two extreme courses, it might in one way or another insist on or assist in the prevention of pollution upstream, finding the required resources by imposing a tax on the collectivity of the two communities. In this compromise, it would be acting partly as an intermediary and partly as a senior government adopting a national point of view.

In summary, it appears that. the problem of the distribution of jurisdiction between neighbouring communities should be analysed by benefit-cost analysis only when a senior level of government is prepared on political grounds to adopt a national point of view, especially under circumstances of known high factor mobility. If a national point of view is not acceptable, then benefit-cost procedures must give way to inter-jurisdictional bargaining – perhaps through the intermediation of a senior government.

C. *The distribution of tastes*

The control of pollution epitomizes problems about tastes which are presumably present in all public decisions but are rarely recognized. We refer to the fact that the assessment of benefits from pollution control depends upon whether or not people have become accustomed to the environment in which they live. Again, attitudes to the imposition of costs for the purification of pollution (say upon the producers of effluents) depend upon whether such producers believe that they are despoiling an otherwise pure environment or whether they believe that they have a perfect moral right to make use of the atmosphere or water courses for their discharges.

We may offer one or two hypothetical examples. People living in a rural environment who are suddenly enveloped in smoke from a new factory will presumably place the benefits of the smoke's removal at a much higher figure than those living in the city who are already accustomed to being the target of arbitrarily placed discharges. Indeed, in the latter circumstances people may have grown up in an entirely impure environment and think little or nothing of it. In such circumstances, an accurate benefit-cost analysis would have to conclude that the personal benefits of pollution control were negligible.

Alternatively, consider the imposition of the costs of pollution control. The owners of a new factory in a smoke-ridden city may fiercely resent a ruling that they must prevent the discharge of wastes by expensive methods. However, the owners of the same factory placed beside a bathing beach might think it quite reasonable that local authorities would wish to prevent them from polluting a recreational area.

These examples illustrate the point that the estimate of benefits and costs under benefit-cost procedures is largely a subjective matter based upon what people like and particularly upon what they have become accustomed to. Thus, just as in the previous section it appeared that the validity of benefit-cost results depends on the point of view being adopted, here the validity is shown to depend upon whose tastes are being consulted in the estimation of dollar values.

At the one extreme we have those who believe that the environment should have attributed to it a norm close to that of a prehistoric state of nature. Anyone who alters this environment is reducing such people's enjoyment so that benefits will clearly result from projects which would tend to restore the environmental state of nature. On the other hand, we have those who would take the existing state of environment as the norm and would measure benefits and costs as the value of small changes from this level. Benefit-cost procedures conducted from this point of view are obviously likely to result in few positive recommendations for environmental change; whereas the first extreme view is likely to discover huge benefits in environmental changes.

Economists can offer little guidance on this matter but merely act as interested observers. They are aware that when income distribution problems arise (section A) it is customary to work from the existing distribution of income. This has been called the unacceptable value judgment of welfare economics which accepts the status quo distribution of income as a measure of the relative strength of feeling of different individuals. Symmetrically, economists should avoid making an implicit value judgment in taking current tastes about the state of the environment as given. Who knows how people will feel in one hundred years about the removal of pollution? If the quality of the environment has been degraded in the meantime, society may have come to accept this new state of nature, just as Oriental societies now accept high population densities. If, on the other hand, pollution has been markedly abated, society may feel that any threat to the purity of the environment must be resisted, even at very high costs.

A useful way of considering this question is to distinguish between present and potential benefit. Present benefit from an unpolluted environment to a person conditioned to a polluted one may be very small, but his potential benefit, allowing for his experiencing and cultivation of the amenities of an unpolluted environment, may be large. It can be argued that it is the potential rather than the present benefit that is relevant in benefit-cost analysis. Perhaps the terms "short-run" and "long-run" would be preferable to "present" and "potential."

Another somewhat similar line of argument is that one of the aims of society is, or should be, to improve itself — to raise the level of its tastes — and that this improvement will not be brought about except by leadership of a discriminating minority whose judgment is condoned by the majority. This may apply even to goods that will never appeal directly to or be enjoyed by more than a small minority, even though the vast majority take pride in its existence. Most "cultural" services are of this nature — public art galleries, state operas, perhaps the CBC, etc. Pollution control might be justified on the same basis where the majority of a people are not directly aware of its benefits. In this case it is likely that they will also come to appreciate and value them if given the opportunity.

Our inclination in this matter is to promote the moral judgment that people who do not put a high value upon a pure environment are usually the people who have not experienced one. Being infected by the very disease which the analysis is examining, their evaluation of benefits and costs may have to be accepted only with qualifications, or given low weight. We are therefore arguing that the value judgments which should be accepted are those of the fresh-air and pure-water fraternity. But, we repeat, this is merely our personal moral judgment.

CONCLUSION

Our investigation of these three distributional circumstances is not meant to invalidate the use of benefit-cost procedures in deciding upon pollution control measures. Far from it. Indeed, we have emphasized that to a greater or lesser extent these distribution circumstances exist in any economic evaluation procedure of any large indivisible project.

However, we have stressed that environmental pollution problems frequently confront these distributional circumstances to an extended degree. Therefore, those who are making the benefit-cost calculations ought to be sensitive to the "whose ox is gored?" question before coming to strong conclusions. Furthermore, it behoves them to ask whether the estimate of benefits which they are using is based upon present (short-run) tastes or potential (long-run) tastes.

1 See John F. Graham, "Fiscal Adjustments in a Federal Country," in
   Inter-governmental Fiscal Relationships, Canadian Tax Paper 40 (Toronto:
   Canadian Tax Foundation, 1964).
2 John F. Graham, "Fiscal Adjustment and Economic Development: A Case
   Study of Nova Scotia" (Toronto: University of Toronto Press, 1963), and
   A.D. Scott, "The Economic Goals of Federal Finance," *Public Finance,*
   1964, pp. 241-88.

Economic incentives in air pollution control

Air pollution can be controlled or eliminated by three types of public policy: direct regulation, payments by the government to assist in reducing pollution, and effluent taxes. In the following article from *The Economics of Air Pollution* edited by H. Wolozin (New York: W.W. Norton, 1966), Edwin Mills discusses the repercussions of these three measures on prices, output, and resource allocation in the economy. He concludes that a discharge or effluent fee is the best method available to control pollution and illustrates how this might operate.

Smoke is one of the classic examples of external diseconomies mentioned in the writings of Alfred Marshall and his followers. Generations of college instructors have used this form of air pollution as an illustration to help their students to understand conditions under which competitive markets will or will not allocate resources efficiently. By now, the theoretical problems have been explored with the sharpest tools available to economists. The consensus among economists on the basic issue is overwhelming, and I suspect one would be hard-pressed to find a proposition that commands more widespread agreement among economists than the following. The discharge of pollutants into the atmosphere imposes on some members of society costs which are inadequately imputed to the sources of the pollution by free markets, resulting in more pollution than would be desirable from the point of view of society as a whole.

In spite of the widespread agreement on the fundamental issues regarding externalities such as air pollution, there have been remarkably few attempts in the scholarly literature to carry the analysis beyond this point. Most writers have been content to point out that the free market will misallocate resources in this respect, and to conclude that this justifies intervention. But what sort of intervention? There are many kinds, and some are clearly preferable to others.

Too often we use the imperfect working of a free market to justify *any* kind of intervention. This is really an anomalous situation. After all, markets are man-made institutions, and they can be designed in many ways. When an economist concludes that a free market is working badly — giving the wrong signals, so to speak — he should also ask how the market may be restructured so that it will give the right signals.

Thus, in the case of air pollution, acceptance of the proposition stated above leads most people to think entirely in terms of direct regulation — permits, registration, licenses, enforcement of standards and so on. I submit that this is rather like abandoning a car because it has a flat tire. Of course, in some cases the car may be working so badly that the presence of a flat tire makes it rational to abandon it, and correspondingly the inadequacies of some market mechanisms may make abandonment desirable. Nevertheless, I submit that the more logical procedure is to ask how a badly functioning market may be restructured to preserve the clear advantages of free and decentralized decision-making, but to remedy its defects. Only when there appears to be no feasible way of structuring a market so that it will give participants the right signals, should it be given up in favor of direct regulation.

It is easy to state the principle by which the socially desirable amount of pollution abatement should be determined: *Any given pollution level should be reached by the least costly combination of means available; the level of pollution should be achieved at which the cost of a further reduction would exceed the benefits.*

To clothe the bare bones of this principle with the flesh of substance is a very tall order indeed. In principle, if every relevant number were known, an edict could be issued to each polluter specifying the amount by which he was to reduce his discharge of pollutants and the means by which he was to do so. In fact, we are even farther from having the right numbers for air pollution than we are from having those for water pollution.

In this situation, I suggest that any scheme for abatement should be consistent with the following principles:

1. It should permit decision-making to be as decentralized as possible. Other things being equal, a rule that discharges must be reduced by a certain amount is preferable to a rule that particular devices be installed, since the former permits alternatives to be considered that may be cheaper than the devices specified in the latter.

2. It should be experimental and flexible. As experience with abatement schemes accumulates, we will gain information about benefits and costs of abatement. We will then revise our ideas about the desirable amount and methods of abatement. Control schemes will have to be revised accordingly.

3. It should be coupled with careful economic research on benefits and costs of air-pollution abatement. Without benefit-cost calculations, we cannot determine the desirable amount of abatement. We can, however, conjecture with confidence that more abatement is desirable than is provided by existing controls. Therefore, our present ignorance of benefits and costs should not be used as an excuse for doing nothing. I would place great emphasis on doing the appropriate research as part of any control scheme. A well-designed scheme will provide information (e.g., on the costs of a variety of control devices) that is relevant to the benefit-cost calculations.

MEANS OF CONTROL

We are not in a position to evaluate a variety of schemes that are in use or have been proposed to control or abate air pollution. It will be useful to classify methods of control according to the categories employed by Kneese in his discussion of water pollution:

1. Direct regulation. In this category, I include licenses, permits, compulsory standards, zoning, registration, and equity litigation.

2. Payments. In this category I include not only direct payments or subsidies, but also reductions in collections that would otherwise be made. Examples are subsidization of particular control devices, forgiveness of local property taxes on pollution-control equipment, accelerated depreciation on control equipment, payments for decreases in the discharge of pollutants, and tax credits for investment in control equipment.

3. Charges. This category includes schedules of charges or fees for the discharge of different amounts of specified pollutants and excise or other taxes on specific sources of pollution (such as coal).

My objection to direct regulation should be clear by now. It is too rigid and inflexible, and loses the advantages of decentralized decision-making. For example, a rule that factories limit their discharges of pollutants to certain levels would be less desirable than a system of effluent fees that achieved the same overall reduction in pollution, in that the latter would permit each firm to make the adjustment to the extent and in the manner that best suited its own situation. Direct restrictions are usually cumbersome to administer, and rarely achieve more than the grossest form of control. In spite of the fact that almost all of our present control programs fall into this category, they should be tried only after all others have been found unworkable.

Thus, first consideration ought to be given to control schemes under the second and third categories.

Many of the specific schemes under these two categories are undesirable in that they involve charges or payments for the wrong thing. If it is desired to reduce air pollution, then the charge or payment should depend on the amount of pollutants discharged and not on an activity that is directly or indirectly related to the discharge of pollutants. For example, an excise tax on coal is less desirable than a tax on the discharge of pollutants resulting from burning coal because the former distorts resource use in favor of other fuels and against devices to remove pollutants from stack gases after burning coal. As a second example, a payment to firms for decreasing the discharge of pollutants is better than a tax credit for investment in pollution-control devices because the latter introduces a bias against other means of reducing the discharge of pollutants, such as the burning of nonpolluting fuels. Thus, many control schemes can be eliminated on the principle that more efficient control can normally be obtained by incentives that depend on the variable it is desired to influence rather than by incentives that depend on a related variable.

Many of the specific schemes under "Payments" can be eliminated on the grounds that they propose to subsidize the purchase of devices that neither add to revenues nor reduce costs. Thus, if a pollution-control device neither helps to produce salable products nor reduces production costs, a firm really receives very little incentive to buy the device even if the government offers to pay half the cost. All that such subsidy schemes accomplish is to reduce somewhat the resistance to direct controls. Of course, some control devices may help to recover wastes that can be made into salable products. Although there are isolated examples of the recovery of valuable wastes in the process of air-pollution control, it is hard to know whether such possibilities are extensive. A careful survey of this subject would be interesting. However, the key point is that, to the extent that waste recovery is desirable, firms receive the appropriate incentive to recover wastes by the use of fees or payments that are related to the discharge of effluents. Therefore, even the possibility of waste recovery does not justify subsidization of devices to recover wastes.

The foregoing analysis creates a presumption in favor of schemes under which either payments are made for reducing the discharge of pollutants or charges are made for the amount of pollutants discharged. The basic condition for optimum resource allocation can in principle be satisfied by either scheme, since under either scheme just enough incentive can be provided so that the marginal cost of further abatement approximates the marginal benefits of further abatement. There are, however, three reasons for believing that charges are preferable to subsidies:

1. There is no natural "origin" for payments. In principle, the payment should be for a reduction in the discharge of pollutants below

what it would have been without the payment. Estimation of this magnitude would be difficult and the recipient of the subsidy would have an obvious incentive to exaggerate the amount of pollutants he would have discharged without the subsidy. The establishment of a new factory would raise a particularly difficult problem. The trouble is precisely that which agricultural policy meets when it tries to pay farmers to reduce their crops. Jokes about farmers deciding to double the amount of corn not produced this year capture the essence of the problem.

2. Payments violate feelings of equity which many people have on this subject. People feel that if polluting the air is a cost of producing certain products, then the consumers who benefit ought to pay this cost just as they ought to pay the costs of labor and other inputs needed in production.

3. If the tax system is used to make the payments, e.g., by permitting a credit against tax liability for reduced discharge of pollutants, a "gimmick" is introduced into the tax system which, other things being equal, it is better to avoid. Whether or not the tax system is used to make the payments, the money must be raised at least partly by higher taxes than otherwise for some taxpayers. Since most of our taxes are not neutral, resource misallocation may result.

I feel that the above analysis creates at least a strong presumption for the use of discharge or effluent fees as a means of air-pollution abatement.

Briefly, the proposal is that air pollution control authorities be created with responsibility to evaluate a variety of abatement schemes, to estimate benefits and costs, to render technical assistance, to levy charges for the discharge of effluents, and to adopt other means of abatement.

Serious problems of air pollution are found mostly in urban areas of substantial size. Within an urban area, air pollution is no respecter of political boundaries, and an authority's jurisdiction should be defined by the boundaries of a metropolitan air shed . . . In a number of instances, the authority would have to be interstate. In many large metropolitan areas, the authority would have to be the joint creation of several local governments. There would presumably be participation by state governments and by the federal government at least to the extent of encouragement and financial support.

Each authority would have broad responsibility for dealing with air pollution in its metropolitan air shed. It would institute discharge fees and would be mainly financed by such fees. It would have the responsibility of estimating benefits and costs of air-pollution abatement, and of setting fees accordingly. It would have to identify major pollutants in its area and set fees appropriate to each significant pollutant. The authority could also provide technical advice and help concerning methods of abatement.

Although there would be great uncertainty as to the appropriate level of fees at first, this should not prevent their use. They should be set conservatively while study was in progress, and data on the ro sponses of firms to modest fees would be valuable in making benefit-cost calculations. Given present uncertainties, a certain amount of flexible experimentation with fees would be desirable.

Questions will necessarily arise as to just what kinds and sources of pollutants would come under the jurisdiction of the proposed authority. I do not pretend to have answers to all such questions. Presumably, standard charges could be set for all major pollutants, with provision for variation in each metropolitan air shed to meet local conditions. It is clear that provision should be made for the possibility of varying the charge for a particular pollutant from air shed to air shed. The harm done by the discharge of a ton of sulfur dioxide will vary from place to place, depending on meteorological and other factors. It is probably less harmful in Omaha than in Los Angeles. It is important that charges reflect these differences, so that locational decisions will be appropriately affected.

Consideration would also have to be given to the appropriate temporal pattern of charges. In most cities, pollution is much more serious in summer than at other times. Charges that were in effect only during summer months might induce a quite different set of adjustments than charges that were in effect at all times.

No one should pretend that the administration of an effective air-pollution control scheme will be simple or cheap. Measurement and monitoring of discharges are necessary under any control scheme and can be expensive and technically difficult. Likewise, whatever the control scheme, finding the optimum degree of abatement requires the calculation of benefits and costs; these calculations are conceptually difficult and demanding.

The point that needs to be emphasized strongly is that the cost of administering a control scheme based on effluent fees will be less than the cost of administering any other scheme of equal effectiveness. An effluent-fee system, like ordinary price systems, is largely self-administering.

This point is important and is worth stating in detail. First, consider an effluent-fee system. Suppose a schedule of fees has been set. Then firms will gradually learn the rate of effluent discharge that is most profitable. Meanwhile, the enforcement agency will need to sample the firm's effluent to ensure that the firm is paying the fee for the amount actually discharged. However, once the firm has found the most profitable rate of effluent discharge, and this is known to the enforcing agency, the firm will have no incentive to discharge any amount of effluent other than the one for which it is paying. At this point the system becomes self-administering and the enforcement agency need only collect bills. Second, consider a regulatory scheme under which the permissible discharge is set at the level that actually resulted under the effluent-fee scheme. Then the firm has a continuing incentive because of its advantage on the cost side to exceed the permissible discharge rate so as to increase production. Monitoring by the enforcement agency therefore continues to be necessary.

Of course, under either a regulatory or an effluent-fee scheme, a change in conditions will require the search for a new "equilibrium." Neither system can be self-enforcing until the new equilibrium has been found. The point is that the effluent-fee system becomes self-enforcing at that point, whereas the regulatory system does not.

Some fiscal aspects of controlling industrial water pollution[*]

There are a number of methods which governments can use to reduce water pollution such as regulations, assistance in developing abatement programs, and effluent charges. Each of these raises a number of questions about economic efficiency, administrative feasibility, and fairness, according to certain social values. In the following contribution, Richard M. Bird and Leonard Waverman of the University of Toronto examine these various methods of control in some detail, indicating the conditions where one method may prove superior to others.

[*] This paper is based on one originally prepared by Bird in 1967. It has been updated and revised for publication in the present form with the help of Waverman and an Isaak Walton Killam award from the Canada Council.

Environmental pollution has in recent years become a subject of great public interest.[1] Many public policies have been proposed to control pollution and to improve the quality of man's environment. Some of these proposals have been implemented. No student of public policy will be surprised to learn that many of these policy measures involve the use of the fiscal system in one way or another. The first political reaction to a newly perceived need such as that for pollution control is probably to impose negative direct controls: "Thou shalt not" dump sewage into lakes from pleasure boats, build cottages without adequate sewage disposal facilities, burn coal with high sulphur content, and so on. But it usually becomes quickly apparent that absolute prohibition is inefficient since it unrealistically imputes an infinite social cost to the addition of one more unit of pollutant to the already polluted environment. It also does not help much in correcting the detrimental effects on environmental quality of the big pollutors in large urban concentrations and certain major industries (including agriculture). Direct controls are certainly needed in any thorough-going pollution control program, but they cannot do the job alone. Direct government expenditures, indirect expenditures (through loan programs or the tax system), or positive taxes are therefore prominent features of most pollution abatement programs. Since much economic analysis in recent years has made it plain that some form of effluent charge or similar pricing device is probably the best all-round technique of bringing about pollution abatement, we shall here focus on other fiscal measures. The purpose of this paper, then, is to survey in a preliminary fashion the possible role of fiscal instruments — particularly grants to municipalities and tax incentives — in the control and abatement of water pollution, especially that arising from the activities of non-agricultural industry.

The paper is organized in three principal sections. First, there is a brief introductory discussion of the economics and politics of pollution control in order to establish a framework for the subsequent analysis of particular fiscal measures. Fortunately, it is not necessary to treat either these "big" questions or the complex technology of pollution abatement in detail in order to analyse the probable efficacy of the fiscal instruments we shall discuss.[2] The second main section of the paper is concerned with fiscal aspects of intergovernmental relations, and the third treats the question of fiscal measures in relation to the private sector. Some reference to existing and proposed

Canadian legislation is made from time to time for illustrative purposes, but we have not attempted to depict the rapidly changing legal situation in detail. Our main aim in this paper is to sketch the policy directions indicated by economic analysis, rather than to provide a critique of the policies on which major reliance is apparently to be placed in Canada. If, however, the reader emerges from this discussion with some doubts about the usefulness of certain widely employed policies intended to foster the abatement of industrial water pollution, our purpose will be well served.

PART I   THE ECONOMICS AND POLITICS OF CONTROLLING
WATER POLLUTION

Pollution is an economic, not a moral problem. There is no conspiracy of evil pollutors trying to do us all in. We, all of us, are the pollutors. Sometimes we pollute the water through the action or inaction of economic agents (business firms), sometimes through political agents (local governments), and sometimes we do it ourselves. Pollution is thus generally an undesired by-product of the process of producing something we want, whether it be cheap paper, low-cost sewage facilities in cities, or inexpensive summer cottages. Dirty water is part of the price we pay for these goods and services. Furthermore, it may well be, in many instances, a price worth paying; although the calculation of the price is not now being made. The economic problem is thus that our economic and political system fails to take this part of the cost of production explicitly into account in making production decisions. This failure leads to a divergence between private and social costs and hence to an inefficient allocation of scarce resources.

It is most unlikely that the economically efficient solution will require the elimination of all water pollution. Our choice is not "clean water" or "dirty water." Rather we have to decide what level of dirt best accords with the nature and quantity of the resources available to us (including clean water) and the nature and variety of the demands we are attempting to satisfy with them.[3] From this standpoint, then, the most efficient combination of pollution control methods is certain to be complex, for the problem of pollution itself is complex and multi-faceted. The problems in determining the exact nature of this efficient combination are not really conceptual but practical.

The major problem in organizing fiscal and other policy instruments to achieve pollution control is the severe practical difficulty of obtaining information and of measuring the costs and benefits of different abatement techniques in situations in which the relevant prices cannot be observed, and people cannot be relied upon to tell the truth.[4] The informational and organizational costs of alternative solutions to pollution are thus crucial determinants of the best package of control measures in any given situation.

In the real world, however, discussion of pollution control often proceeds as though there were severe conceptual as well as practical difficulties in determining the best combination of methods to be used. Two factors give rise to most of the confusing discussion on these matters: the first is equity and the second is the existence of different political jurisdictions. What is "equitable" or "inequitable" is, of course, not a question that the economist as an economist can answer, so all we want to do here is to note a few obvious points. First, the redistributional effects of any pollution control measure are difficult to discern, since the point in the "production and waste"— "consumption and waste" cycle at which the impact of a measure is felt bears no necessary relation to the point at which it has its final incidence in the form of affecting the distribution of real incomes. Incidence depends on the complex interactions through market processes on both the sources and uses side of income.

Second, as a general principle of economic policy, attempts to achieve distributional objectives through interventions in resource allocation are usually inefficient in terms of both allocational and distributional goals. Direct income transfers are therefore the preferred means of offsetting any undesired effects of pollution control measures on income distribution, whether interpersonal or interregional. If for some reason, such transfers cannot be made, the cost in lessened efficiency that will be paid by attempting to compensate through varying the control structure must be recognised.

Third, the notion of "interfirm equity" is meaningless philosophically since firms are not people. The effects of alternative control policies on different firms are therefore better analysed in terms of economic efficiency than of some vague notion of equity. This point is especially important if it is decided to employ tax incentives as part of a comprehensive pollution control policy. The principal reason why any incentives are necessary is indeed likely to be the rather fuzzy view that it is "unfair" to expect existing firms to adopt new standards overnight. It is hard to see any "equity" aspect to this problem, since life is full of upsets (government-induced or otherwise), but the political weight of such arguments may be strong.

As the table on p. 43 points out, there are few inhabited areas of this country which do not suffer from some form of water pollution, be it municipal or industrial.[5] The presence of widespread water pollution does not itself, however, necessitate federal action. Pollution is, in the nature of water systems, always localized so that the type and severity of pollution differs from water basin to water basin. To have the federal government finance all forms of pollution reduction and abatement projects would likely involve the subsidization of cleaning costs for areas with high pollution by areas with low pollution. There is no equity in having residents of some mountain region who long ago installed strict pollution prevention laws subsidize the cleansing of water in some distant heavily polluted metropolis whose residents (usually implicitly) chose low taxes over low pollution. If pollution problems are by nature at most area-wide, and not national in scope, why is there a need for federal action?[6]

Three arguments – the fragmented nature of local government structures, the spillover of costs and benefits to more than one municipality, and municipal competition for industry – are normally given as proof that municipalities (and provinces?) acting alone will tend to overpollute and hence federal intervention is necessary.

There is no doubt that the local government structure in many metropolitan areas is fragmented. Since the need to abate pollution seems to occur mainly in, or near, metropolitan areas, the solution of the pollution problem has occasionally been thought to be the same as the solution of such other pressing metropolitan problems as urban transportation and land-use planning – namely, through some sort of metropolitan or regional government, limited or general, unitary or federal, but in any event covering a wide enough area to internalize the relevant externalities.

It is true that if local governments cannot or will not do the job of pollution control because most of the benefits are felt outside their boundaries or because the cost of operating treatment facilities on the scale needed is prohibitive for one local authority alone, then indeed one cannot rely only on local government to do the job. In these circumstances, there will be substantial underinvestment in pollution control facilities simply because of the inappropriate organization of local government structure in the affected areas.

This fact, however, does not explain why the federal government needs to enter the picture at all. Why don't the affected local governments simply band together in a geographically adequate unit to realize economies of scale and to appropriate most of the benefits from the investment? In fact, they can do and have done just this in some instances. If the local authorities themselves are too apathetic, too unaware of their own best interests, or too hard up to do anything, the provincial government surely can and should. In fact, this has been the preferred pattern in the relatively few efforts made at pollution control in Canada up to now (all provinces have some kind of agency responsible for water quality in the province), and properly so, as far as technical considerations are concerned. For the relatively few important instances where the drainage basin crosses provincial boundaries, special interprovincial (or, in the case of the Great Lakes, international) pollution control authorities can and should be set up to deal with the problem. Again, this is the pattern that has in fact often been followed.

In short, so far as the argument has taken us to this point, it appears that what is required to combat water pollution is an area-wide effort, seldom above the level of one or two provinces in scope and, indeed, rarely outside the boundaries of a single province. Until recently, there has been no compelling federal interest in pure water if the people in the areas with dirty water like it that way. It may be, for example, that citizens of poor areas with clean water would prefer to be richer and dirtier: this is, after all, the choice which most industrial areas made in the past. Is this path to "progress" to be barred by national prohibition? If the choice is made from ignorance of the costs of industralization, national propaganda may be called for, but not necessarily national money.

The central point here is that the benefits of investment in the control of water pollution are geographically limited. On grounds of equity and efficiency there seems every reason to want the investment to be financed by those who benefit (we assume that the distributional aim of public finance is met at the national, not the local, level).[7] The financing possibilities of provinces and municipalities may be circumscribed, but they are not absent. There therefore appears to be no pressing economic, welfare, or political reason for substantial federal intervention in this problem, unless its nature has been completely misspecified here. On all these grounds the case for federal intervention is much stronger with respect to, for example, primary school education, hospitals, public welfare, or almost any human resource activity, than it is with respect to the control of water pollution.

Nevertheless, there is one substantial problem on which the case for federal activity in this field rests. This is the competition between cities and provinces for industry. So long as there is such competition, as there clearly is today, local initiative, even at the regional or provincial level, cannot be relied upon to resolve the pollution problem. Each municipality and province will be afraid that if it alone enforces a rigorous anti-pollution code, imposes effluent charges or equivalent user charges on industrial wastes discharged into municipal systems, or simply levies the other taxes that would be necessary to finance a central treatment system from general revenues, it will reduce its attractiveness to industry and thus lose tax base. A lower tax base means a higher tax rate will be necessary to supply a given level of public services than in the low-pollution-standard areas to which the (short-sighted?) industries might flee, so that the high-standard areas become still less attractive, and so on. Tax flight is thus a cumulative process. Sustained competitive non-enforcement of this sort would presumably disappear over time as the whole country became equally industrialized and/or polluted, but this consideration seems too utopian to enter the decision functions of hard-pressed provincial and municipal authorities. Fear of losing industry is particularly marked in older industrialized areas whose population has a high demand for other public services. These are usually the very areas where pollution is at its worst. It is fundamentally this problem, of interjurisdictional competition for tax base, which requires a federal role in solving the problem.

Federal Role in Water Pollution Control

One particular area in which more federal work is clearly needed is in the adoption of standards of water quality. The Canada Water Act (see Appendix) sets the stage for this task, which requires not only technical work in drawing up the standards, but considerable consultation with the provincial and other enforcing authorities in order to get them to adopt suitably related standards. Even more important, and difficult, is to get these standards enforced. In addition to technical aid and political and administrative consultation and co-operation on this problem, it would seem a reasonable and desirable requirement of any aid to subnational governments that those bodies receiving the aid have acceptable standards and enforce them effectively, subject of course to the transitional problems (which would sometimes be enormous) of converting to the new standards. Examples of appropriate tests might be the prohibition of new sources of industrial pollution unless they are consistent with the water quality management plan (see below), the control of problems arising from inadequate individual waste-treatment facilities in subdivisions, and the like.

In other words, financial assistance should be directed primarily towards the correction of old evils, and a condition of receiving the assistance should be the prevention of major new evils. The direct exercise of federal authority through the Fisheries Act, the Navigable Waters Protection Act, and so on, and the use of pressure through federal contracts, supplements but cannot replace this condition. The general problems of interprovincial differences in fiscal capacity and seriousness of pollution would cause confusion, but these problems might best be resolved as suggested in the subsequent discussion on intergovernmental fiscal relations.

Further, it may perhaps be argued that co-operation between jurisdictions in imposing relatively uniform standards, if this is thought necessary to deflate the competition argument, can come only from federal intervention, owing to the widely varying nature of the problem in different parts of the country (a point used earlier to indicate its non-federal character). The economically efficient system of marked non-uniformity in control measures, to match the inherent non-uniformity of the problem, is thus offset in part by the political requirement of substantial uniformity in order to reduce socially unprofitable competition for industries. At most, however, this argument justifies some minimal federal assistance to local pollution control boards or the federal establishment of minimum purity standards and not anything as drastic as federal assumption of the function, or even full control of local efforts.

The federal role should, it appears, be limited to getting relatively uniform standards agreed upon — no doubt sweetening the process with some transfer of funds — and secondarily to ease the loss felt in competitive position in those areas in which either the pollution problem is most serious or the selling of the right to pollute is a major locational asset. How this might best be done is the subject of the remainder of this paper.[8]

The introduction of minimum water quality standards will require that certain municipalities and industries bear very heavy capital and operating costs in order to meet these effluent standards.[9] The question of whether some transitional assistance should be offered to these industries and municipalities is a difficult one to answer. On one hand, the polluting municipalities chose heavy pollution over low taxes and less industry. The municipality alone should therefore pay for its sins. Likewise, the polluting industry chose to offer its goods at a lower price rather than paying the costs of waste emission, so it alone should pay for emission controls by raising the price of the goods. On the other hand, many of the polluting municipalities and industries began to discharge their wastes many years ago when there was no excess demand for clean water. Should these firms and areas bear heavy costs just because other firms have raised the level of pollutants to harmful levels?

Disregarding this question of ultimate responsibility, the fact must be faced that the establishment of effective standards will have a profound effect on the costs of certain industries and municipalities, leading to substantial impacts on labour markets and municipal tax rates. It may be preferable to prevent serious short-run dislocations of markets by offering temporary financial assistance. Assistance must be temporary; otherwise the pollutor will still not pay for the damages he causes while the rest of us will, through higher taxes rather than through cleaning bills or illness. In the following discussion of fiscal instruments, the transitional nature of each policy will be highlighted.

PART II   INTERGOVERNMENTAL FISCAL RELATIONS

Direct Federal Provision of Facilities

One way to reduce industrial pollution of water in some instances is to channel industrial liquid wastes through municipal sewage treatment facilities, after initial treatment by industry to remove impurities which the municipal systems are not designed to handle. If it is decided, for technical or other reasons, to follow this path in some localities, the appropriate form of any federal assistance to subnational governments ought presumably to be decided along the lines sketched above. For example, apart from cleaning its own stables (for example, in military installations), there seems no reason why the federal government should even contemplate direct federal provision of water pollution abatement facilities, so this alternative can be discarded at once.

The alternative of federal or provincial construction of facilities and subsequent leasing to local governments or authorities would amount to a complete subsidy on capital costs, with the municipality bearing only the operating costs. The major problems with this procedure are that the higher levels of government would be inappropriately involved in detailed decision-making on the scale and type of facility needed at the local level and that, as previously suggested, there seems no reason why taxpayers as a whole should bear the main burden of resolving these essentially localized problems.[10]

Loan Assistance

If it is in raising the necessary capital that the big roadblock to more adequate local investment in sewage treatment facilities exists (apart from the demand factors mentioned earlier), then there are various ways in which the federal government by itself, or, better (since the municipalities are creatures of the provinces), together with the provinces can provide capital assistance. Loans to municipal governments for this purpose from private sources or the flotation of bond issues might, for instance, be guaranteed by the federal and/or provincial governments, thus presumably increasing their quality and acceptability and lowering the interest cost — at no cost to the higher level of government, if one ignores the possibility of the failure of an issue or of offsetting upward pressure on other bond issues. Technical assistance and information on the intricacies of the municipal bond market could be provided to the smaller authorities and sewage disposal districts which will likely be most in need of it. All these measures would cost little and could presumably be of some help.[11]

These mundane measures are too useful to be lost sight of in the present rush for more glamorous (and expensive) solutions. The fact that whatever is done to improve municipal borrowing capacity is more likely to help large than small authorities is no objection, since areas in which large authorities are likely to have to be created (if they do not now exist) are those which on the whole tend to have serious pollution problems.

More direct assistance to municipalities could be provided by federal or provincial loans. At present, for example, the National Housing Act as administered by the Central Mortgage and Housing Corporation will advance two-thirds of the cost of construction of sewage treatment plants and main sanitary sewers for approved municipal projects. Between 1960 and 1968, $272 million was lent in this way for 1381 projects in 905 municipalities.[12] Similarly, in Ontario, the provincial water quality agency (the Ontario Water Resources Commission) had, by 1968, lent around $800 million dollars to Ontario municipalities for sewage treatment and disposal facilities.[13]

Loans might be granted either on the basis of request or to those areas most adversely affected by uniform tightening-up of water quality standards and enforcement. Cheap, readily available loans in the transition period would seem a suitable instrument for facilitating required compliance. Indeed, in some ways, loan finance would appear to be more suitable than grants-in-aid, since loans stress the transitional, "over-the-hump" nature of the federal financial role and, over time, will permit the entire cost of the facilities to be borne by those who benefit. The extent of subsidy in loans may, of course, be varied within a wide range to meet over-all cost constraints on assistance for water pollution abatement and to some extent to deal with the differences in different areas arising from differences in the seriousness of the problem of pollution and in the fiscal capacity of the relevant subnational governments. These problems are discussed further below in connection with grants. Loans to private industry are discussed in the next section.

Other Federal Assistance

There seems to be no case at all for specific national government financial assistance on the operating costs of facilities once constructed.

On the other hand, if there is at the present time — owing, for example, to the lack of effective demand in the past — a shortage of training facilities for sanitary engineers or some other transitional roadblock to wider public sector activity in this field, then federal assistance in setting up and running such training facilities would be quite appropriate. The same holds true for federal technical assistance on pollution problems to the provinces and localities (and industry) and for research and development of new techniques for handling waste. The lag of efforts in these fields in the past provides adequate justification for such activity, and an expanded direct federal role in these fields is probably necessary if much is to be done about water pollution abatement in the near future. It is not really possible, however, to set any price tag on how much of this activity should be undertaken or what its exact nature should be other than through the normal messy and imperfect (even with program budgeting and cost-benefit analysis) budget procedure by which all such hard questions are decided anyway.

Grants Assistance

What might a program of grants to municipalities for water pollution control look like in the light of the preceding discussion? A number of fundamental questions immediately spring to mind: Should the grants be broad or narrow in scope? Should they focus on stimulation or equalization? How should they be designed and administered?

It is unlikely that unconditional grants, tax sharing, and similar broad measures will provide much help in this area, for it seems improbable that much of any increase in available financing would be channelled towards the control of water pollution problems for the reasons discussed earlier. However, any increase in provincial and municipal revenues without the necessity of impairing locational competitiveness through higher taxes would remove some of the apparent case for federal concern with the problem. In this limited sense, therefore, such broad schemes might be considered a substitute for narrow federal grants in the waste treatment field, as in some others. If grants meant to help urban areas went to provincial governments, as is likely in the present constitutional setup, and the provinces wanted to resolve the pollution problem, it would be resolved. If they still did not do anything about the pollution problem and — as assumed earlier — a decentralized political system has a positive value in the Canadian context, one might despair, but on the other hand this outcome might simply mean that other things are prized more highly than clean water, perhaps correctly.

Another possibility would be a system of functional or program grants, that is, broad grants conditional on the recipient government meeting certain standards in, for example, the pollution control field, but leaving it up to them how they do it. In many ways this is a most attractive alternative, given the diversity of problems and local situations. However, the apparent preferences of provincial and municipal governments on water are such that most of any relatively unrestricted grant in this field is likely to be spent more on increasing water quantity for municipal and industrial use than on improving water quality.

If the conditions on the grants were made restrictive enough to pin the expenditure down to quality, there is again, it would appear, the informational and political problem of undue centralization of decision-making. But this is not a necessary outcome. Nothing prevents funds being given to provincial governments or appropriate local and regional authorities on condition that (a) an effective anti-pollution law is on the books and being enforced and (b) the funds are used in some broadly acceptable way to improve water quality. If better water is what we are interested in and better water is what we get, to what extent must the federal government specify the way in which we get it? A number of considerations should influence the answer to this question: Who is likely to have the more relevant technical knowledge of local situations? Who is more likely to represent correctly relevant social preferences — the federal government or the provincial and municipal governments? Should federal aid be given on a functional basis directly to operating agencies or should it be channelled through local governments? All these questions need careful consideration in any extension of the present grant (and loan) programs for treatment facilities.

A tentative conclusion might be that, while the general case for more flexibility in intergovernmental fiscal transfers is strong, it is not

particularly strong in the pollution abatement area owing to the past
neglect and the vested interests against change in most polluted areas,
and to the general tendency to underinvest in cleaning up someone
else's water. To get results, it would appear a narrowly defined grant
program is what is really needed. Even so, one should not expect a
great stimulative effect on local spending on this function as a result of
the price-reduction effect of federal aid: the elasticity of demand for
sewage treatment is probably low because of the externalities problem,
so that if much increase in *total* spending is thought necessary it will
have to come about more through direct spending by higher levels of
government than through induced expenditures by *local* governments.
These higher levels, as argued earlier, should be mainly the provinces
and special service agencies, so it might be desirable to tie any federal
grants to some extent to the provision of additional funds by these
levels, whether in the form of loans or grants.

A narrowly defined grant does not, however, necessarily mean one
which is limited to particular types of municipal sewage works. Special
project grants can certainly be useful for demonstration projects and
the like, but requiring detailed approval by the federal government of
every provincial or local move to abate water pollution is not
recommended as the way to a rapid solution of the problem – not to
mention its constitutional improbability in the Canadian setting. A
relatively simple procedure, perhaps allocating grants to provinces
which meet certain criteria (discussed below) and letting the provincial
agencies do the detailed approval work, is probably the best procedure. Local areas in weak provinces (those which cannot or will not
meet the conditions) might be permitted to apply directly to the
federal government, if this is legally possible.

Once a national interest in water pollution is accepted and defined
in terms of water quality standards (or budgetary allocation), it would
seem logical that the first criterion for the allocation of federal funds
between provinces should be the seriousness of the pollution problems
as measured by, for example, population density and the number of
industrial establishments discharging wastes into the water system. It
should be possible to construct an allocation formula along these lines
(or more technically respectable ones) without too much difficulty.
The allocated funds might be distributed as suggested above. If some
province has (in someone's view) a serious pollution problem and no
government level in that province is concerned about it enough to do

anything, it would, of course, get no federal funds under this scheme —
but it is not clear why one should worry about this.

One thing one must worry about, however, is the vast difference in
the fiscal capacity of different areas of the country. Many polluted
areas tend to be wealthy areas, even if local government fragmentation
sometimes keeps the wealth well hidden in the public sector, but
others, especially some old mining areas and the like, are not. Two
things might be done about the equalization problem without undue
damage to the essentially stimulative nature of grants in this field.
First, special programs might be devised for particular areas and
problems — like the sealing of old mines. Second, there should be a
matching requirement in the federal grant scheme which would make
some allowance for differences in fiscal capacity. A common index of
fiscal capacity is some ratio of per capita income, and something like
this would be satisfactory in this case also. (Alternatively, it may be
assumed that differences in fiscal capacity are fully adjusted for by
general regional adjustment grants, so that this factor can be ignored in
the pollution abatement program.)

A poor, badly polluted province would thus receive a large
allocation and have to match the federal money with a relatively small
amount of its own funds; a rich, badly polluted province would also get
a big allocation, but it would have to find more money on its own; and
so on. These suggestions are clearly crude but they seem worthy of
more exploration if in fact federal financing for this purpose is to be
increased. The pattern of grant funds arising from these formulas
would on balance be most unlikely to be progressive in relation to
average provincial per capita income; the reason is simply that the
pollution problem is not progressive and that we have assumed a direct
federal interest in resolving the pollution problem.[14] If clean water is
what is wanted, it is best gotten by cleaning the water where the people
are, not by granting funds to small and poor areas just because they are
small and poor.

As with the equalization problem, so with regional government.
Both more equalization and more regional government may well be
desirable, but setting up water pollution control grants to achieve these
good things is unlikely to achieve these objects and likely to lose some
of the presumably intended effect of improving water quality. Incentives and inducements to local governments to act in their own best
interests and to band together in drainage basin associations can

appropriately be part of any grant legislation, but too much in the way of results should not be expected. Certainly there should be no prejudice against single-purpose special districts: if one purpose is all we are interested in, and we can get local governments to agree on that one purpose, then insisting on multipurpose authorities before they can get grants, as has occasionally been suggested, is indeed foolish. Conversely, if we are interested in encouraging more co-operation at the local level, it should be made easy rather than difficult to qualify for the bonus given to such co-operation. The risk of being hood-winked is surely much smaller than the risk of discouraging such associations through unnecessarily rigid and complex requirements. The tendency to lose sight of the purpose of the incentive must be fought against in grant policy as in tax policy (see below).

One final important point on grant programs, if this is the chosen path to pollution control, needs to be made: periodic reassessments of the program should be required. If a program is supposed to have some effect, it is surely only reasonable to require that it must be demon-strated at reasonable intervals to have that effect and that it should be subject to revision and reshaping by the appropriate agency to achieve its purposes better. (This presumes, as is in fact done throughout this paper, that the objectives of the legislation are clearly specified in meaningful terms, susceptible to analysis – no doubt an idealistic hope, judging from the Canada Water Act. See Appendix.) Further-more, since our concept of the need for federal fiscal assistance at all in this field is that it is temporary (at least in its financial as opposed to training, research, and regulatory aspects), the legislation should have a time limit. For example, a program might be passed in 1971 providing assistance till 1980, subject to reporting and possibly revision of amounts and conditions, say, twice during this ten-year period. Of course, if budgetary or other problems prevent the desired degree of success from being achieved in this period, the program might be re-evaluated and extended at the end of the specified time, but there is real virtue under present conditions in a limited rather than open-ended federal commitment to water pollution control and abatement as a federal responsibility. (The problems of poor areas in coping with this – and all other – responsibilities will, of course, persist, but we assume some more general solution to this will be found by 1990 if not by 1980.)

PART III   FISCAL MEASURES AND THE PRIVATE SECTOR

Many of the techniques outlined in the previous sections might also be used to assist private industry directly. The federal government might, for example, construct facilities and lease them to industrial plants (though this admittedly seems rather fanciful given the specialized nature of much industrial pollution, among other problems) or, more to the point, it could provide information, technical help, some training facilities, and access to credit (either directly or government-guaranteed) for investments in this field. The information, technical, and training assistance would seem as advisable in the private sector as in the public sector, so these activities might well be expanded whatever else is done.

The provision of cheap credit raises other questions, but it introduces no new dimension into government policy and ought to be considered further, especially in comparison with the common proposals for tax incentives.[15] Loans have the desirable characteristic of emphasizing the transitional nature that government assistance ought to have in this field. The principal purpose of government aid is to help convert dirty industrial plants into clean ones; the higher operating cost of the clean plants and, over the long haul, the capital cost too can quite appropriately be borne by the consumers (or producers, depending on the incidence) of the products produced. Private bearing of clean-up costs is, on both equity and efficiency grounds, a more desirable solution than payment by taxpayers. To repeat, then, the case for any government aid to private business for pollution abatement is, at best, a transitional one; and if loans would make this clearer and can be administered properly, the loan alternative ought seriously to be considered. Business, of course, would much prefer some kind of outright gift, or tax incentive, but business preferences should hardly be the deciding consideration.

Another possible solution to the problem of industrial pollution in some instances is for industries to make more use of municipal general sewage treatment facilities. Given the nature of industrial waste, this solution, if artificially encouraged through the provision of substantial central treatment plants and the like, runs the danger of retarding the adoption of economically more sensible ways of reducing industrial pollution at source rather than treating it once it exists. If the rigorous code enforcement suggested below as the *sine qua non* for new plants is carried out, however, the problem would then be reduced to its proper dimensions of concerning only old plants, so it is perhaps less likely that more use of municipal facilities will be distorting. If economies of scale are in fact important in treatment facilities, use of municipal plants might well prove advisable for many small pollutors – the big ones, whose waste water would swamp most municipal plants, are, of course, another story. The best solution probably depends upon precise local conditions – the nature of industrial pollution in the area, the possibility of using existing or expanded municipal facilities economically, and so on. So far as this solution is practical the aids to public bodies discussed in the preceding section will, of course, help the industrial sector. Industrial use of municipal facilities will impose extra costs on the municipalities. While in the short run it might be appropriate for some of these additional costs to be borne by the federal and provincial taxpayers in one of the ways mentioned earlier, for economic efficiency the industry itself should pay these costs, presumably in the form of adequate user charges.

Effluent Charges and Penalties

The procedure now considered advisable by most economists for controlling industrial pollution is somewhat analogous to user charges; it is that effluent charges should be levied in accordance with the pollution degree of industrial waste. Such a system will lead to the desirable quality standard at lowest resource cost. The case for these measures has been argued eloquently and at length elsewhere and will not be repeated here.[16] While effluent charges are in essence a metering device so that firms pay for the pollution they create, penalties (tax or fines) on the other hand are preventive devices. If the firm meets the standard, no penalty is paid. If the firm pollutes at a level just above the standard it pays the same penalty as the firm which grossly pollutes. One difficulty, therefore, is that unless the penalties are set high enough to make it cheaper to meet the quality standard than to pay the penalty, they act like a "licence to pollute" – a politically dangerous phrase – and leave unresolved the problem of how to use the funds thus gathered to clear up the still-polluted water.[17] Faced with a tax penalty on some activity considered socially undesirable, a business has several options: it can pay the tax, meet the standards, go out of business, or move somewhere where there is no penalty. It will presumably choose the most profitable of these courses of action. In theory, therefore, the effects of tax penalties on business activity (and on the quality of water) are indeterminate. In practice, fear of the last two options — going out of business or moving — are likely to preclude the levying in most areas of high enough charges effectively enough enforced to have much success.

Indeed, an excellent parallel to tax penalties in many respects is afforded by the point stressed earlier on the need for more effective code standards and enforcement in any long-term solution to the pollution problem.[18] As far as we can see, there is absolutely no reason why every new industry should not be expected, as from, say, two years from now (some warning time would probably be politically and administratively necessary to avoid disputes about long lead-times in investment plans, etc.) to meet certain nationally uniform standards. The economically efficient alternative of applying controls (or charges) only on plants locating in designated polluted areas may well prove inadvisable in view of likely conflicts with such other national policies as regional development and the interjurisdictional competitive problem. The standards must be more or less nationally uniform, to reiterate, in order to avoid reduction to the lowest common denominator in the competitive battle.

The main problem of new plants concerns the need to get all provinces to adopt approximately the same legislation and to enforce it, assuming that in large part water pollution is and should be a provincial matter. A financial inducement to this end was suggested above. The real problem with codes (or charges) as the solution, however, concerns existing plants. It should be clear by now that this problem is not, except in the most tenuous sense, one of equity: industries that pollute are overexpanded in social terms, and any relative contraction forced by legislation requiring them to meet their full social costs of production is presumably a good thing. The problem is really one of competition for industry and of transitional adjustment.

All adjustments are painful and take time, effort, and money. Adjustments to internalize external diseconomies are no exception. Some alleviation of this pain seems appropriate, just as some offset to these newly imposed private costs is needed to avoid introducing new distortions in industrial location patterns in the short run (some long-term adjustments are to be expected from any of the policies discussed here).

One approach might be to delay application of standards to existing plants for some fixed time, say, five years (or such longer period, not in any circumstances to exceed ten years, as may be negotiated with the appropriate regulatory authority). During this breathing spell, existing plants would be offered financial opportunities to come up to par — loans, grants, tax incentives, or such other inducement as seems necessary. These inducements should be available for some limited period only. After that, all pollutors would be expected to meet minimum essential standards (perhaps these might be set a little more generously for old firms than for new ones in view, among other things, of the likely lower cost of building clean plants in the first place than of fixing up old ones). Its transitional nature is the essential point to keep in mind in designing any efficient policy package.

One possible inducement which deserves brief mention is that of a straight grant to meet part of the cost of investment carried out in order to conform to newly imposed standards of pollution emission. A grant scheme has two distinct advantages over most of the tax incentive schemes that exist or have been proposed: the benefit the firm receives is not dependent on profits (a point which might be especially important for old firms in declining areas), and it can apply to land acquisition and similar costs which would not usually be covered by tax incentives (though they might be redesigned to avoid this problem). Grants similar to those now given to municipalities might also be given directly to industrial firms. There is little precedent in North America for this approach, though it has often been done in, for example, the United Kingdom (the investment grants scheme). The other great advantage of a grant system is that its cost would be obvious to all — a feature not usually appreciated by those on the receiving end, but one which favours rational public expenditure policy.

Grants or explicit subsidies therefore seem preferable on most of the conventional grounds to tax incentives, although we suggest below a few ways in which tax incentives can be made more respectable (essentially by making them more like good grants). The open nature of the grant subsidy is, we assume, preferable to the hidden subsidy now being given to polluting industries, as is its temporary nature.

Tax Incentives

Much of the legislation and discussion of the problems of industrial pollution has been concerned with suggesting different tax incentives. At present, for example, the federal income tax act allows a two-year depreciation of assets acquired between 1965 and 1973 and used for abatement of water pollution. Similarly, Ontario rebates sales tax on pollution abatement devices. Rather than evaluate these and other particular measures in detail, we would like to raise some general issues that should be, but all too seldom are, considered in the design of any tax incentive.

The world is full of problems and even fuller, so it sometimes seems, of those who promise alleviation of these problems at the price of a little tax concession. A basic objection to *any* tax incentive is therefore that giving way on any front, even for something as worthy as pollution control, may open the floodgates to many more exemptions for equally worthy causes and to consequent erosion of the tax base and the elimination of the possibility of rational public expenditure policy.

A second objection is to the hidden cost of tax incentives as usually granted. It is conceptually quite possible, however, to bring out into the open the total of public funds expended in this way as well as information on who receives the benefit. There is no apparent reason why an annual report on the cost to the taxpayer of the incentive program could not be made a part of any new tax incentive in the pollution control field or anywhere else. If the motives of the proponents of these incentives are so weak that they cannot stand even this little light of day, it does not seem likely the incentive will do the country much good.

A third objection is to the possible technological distortion induced by the fact that most of the incentive schemes that have been proposed would limit the benefits to certain kinds of investment. There are, of course, possible problems in this respect (perhaps not only within industrial techniques but also between separate industrial and use of municipal facilities), but it would be easy to overstate the dimensions of the problem. In particular, it is easy to overdo the extent to which we, the government, or anyone else is in fact likely to know in advance what is the least cost solution for each and every pollution abatement problem.

Most tax incentive proposals give benefits only to profitable firms which make specified investments in designated items of treatment equipment or specified kinds of construction. Problems might then arise in two directions: some of the designated equipment may be purchased for uses other than pollution abatement, or some non-designated methods might be more suitable for particular problems but will not be employed because of the tax favouritism to the less efficient method. If the position argued above in favour of transitional assistance only to existing plants is accepted, the outright exemption or favoured treatment of particular items is not suitable because it is too general. It is also not suitable because it is too limited; in particular, because it discriminates against the possible change of industrial processes to reduce pollution. On all accounts, therefore, a different system would seem to be advisable if tax incentives are to be used at all. One possible system might be to limit any tax concession to existing plants and to relate it not to particular forms of investment but to the meeting of certain standards of pollution emission. The required administrative set-up could be something like this: standards would be set and compliance periods specified for each plant by its appropriate local or provincial regulatory authority (this assumes the necessary infrastructure has been set up). Plants could then determine (with government technical help, if necessary) how best to meet the standards, and some concession related to the expenditure certified by the authority as necessary for this purpose could be given. (A similar procedure could be used for grants or loans.)

In other words, an output-based incentive is desirable because it is more closely related to the objective (cleaner water) and because it is freer of technological bias than a cost-based incentive. But the only justification for any incentive is as an aid to transitional adjustment to new standards, and it therefore seems reasonable to relate the incentive to the cost of meeting these standards (or entering the new era of pollution pricing). The main problems here are, of course, the informational one of determining what the appropriate standards are and the political one of establishing them. These difficulties are clearly substantial, but so long as we remember that our concern is only a temporary one and that a fair degree of arbitrariness is inevitable, they are not insuperable.

A few other administrative problems with any incentive scheme, including that sketched immediately above, deserve brief mention. In general, there is no point in putting any tax incentive into the law unless we want people to take advantage of it. We want them to do so presumably because we are interested in the alleviation of some problem by the expenditure induced by the incentive (its stimulative effect is likely to be small unless reinforced by the certainty of effective code enforcement by some specified time, which is another reason for stressing the package nature of the solution). If this is so, the tendency to allow incentives to be installed in the law and then to be emasculated by administrative red tape and inertia — most of it responsive more to the fear of being "taken" into paying for an "unworthy" expenditure than to the "need" for the "worthy" expenditures — must be overcome. The detailed regulation of most tax incentive proposals is all too often more concerned with feared abuses than with ways to make the benefits available to all qualifying expenditures. There is little to be said for tax incentives in general; but if we are to have them in any case, they should be made effectively available.

In addition, the desirability of periodic re-evaluation of any tax incentive program — of a regularly required demonstration of costs and benefits — is as clear as in the previously discussed instance of government grants to municipalities.

The proposal sometimes made to confine the benefits of tax incentives for pollution abatement facilities only to non-revenue-producing facilities is neither desirable nor really workable. The undesirability should be clear from the preceding discussion. If the aim is clean water, what do we care if in the process of cleaning it up someone makes some money? By definition, only basically non-profit-able activities will be undertaken in this field (if they were profitable, ignorance apart, they would have been undertaken already), so any profit is a side product. Such limiting provisions are examples of the undue fear of abuses mentioned above.

On the other hand, it is perfectly conceivable that the best way to clear up some industrial pollution problem would be to build a new plant. Should the government subsidize the whole construction cost in this case (as would seem to be implied by the earlier suggestion on the possibly desirable form of an incentive program)? This is not necessary, provided that the component regulatory authority is empowered to certify (perhaps within some limits) an arbitrary proportion of the investment as being undertaken primarily for the qualifying purpose. Precedent for this procedure, and perhaps other useful lessons as well, may be found in some of the wartime provisions aiding the construction of defence production facilities.

The best form of tax incentive, if this is the chosen route, is an investment credit, related generally to expenditure certified to be undertaken primarily for water pollution abatement. Accelerated depreciation of the sort now in the law has various presumably undesirable distorting effects between firms with different capital intensities, different discount and tax rates, and the like. The constantly heard business refrain that accelerated depreciation is "only" an interest-free loan, however, has little merit, as it (1) ignores the very real benefits of such a loan — available without attention to credit rating — and (2) appears to assume that the business rolls over and dies, never again investing in qualifying assets. This may be true occasionally, especially with a limited scope investment like this, but is likely not the general rule.

A major problem with most tax incentive proposals is that it would be extremely difficult, administratively and politically, to withhold them from new firms, although the logic of the case for any incentives applies only to old ones. The possibility of more and better provincial and local exemptions from property taxes, sales taxes, and income taxes is not worth specific discussion here. The effect of such exemptions is so minor in most cases that the only result is a loss of tax revenue.

Finally, to conclude this admittedly hasty review of a number of points on tax incentives, it must be noted that the psychological effects of incentives may well be more significant than their effects on rates of return or internal liquidity in inducing firms to undertake some desired activity (especially, to repeat, when coupled with the big stick of code enforcement). As someone once said, "if accelerated depreciation will build a blast furnace, it is pointless to insist that it is all done with mirrors." It is unlikely, however that the novelty effect of such now familiar incentives can be counted on to fool many, if any, industrialists these days.

In short, there is not much case for tax incentives for pollution control despite the popularity of such measures. The politics of pollution control may demand that some sort of generous tax incentive be enacted; but the incentive should be, at most, only a transitional part, and not the most important part, of the total policy package required to get very far in this field. If the incentive route is chosen, however, it can be greatly improved by careful and realistic design with the objective of the legislation being kept constantly in mind and with provisions for explicit periodic re-assessment of the program and for explicit annual statements of the costs incurred.

CONCLUSION

Nothing in this paper detracts from the powerful economic case for relying mainly on putting a "price" on pollution thorugh effluent charges, or some similar technique, as the most efficient general approach to reducing industrial water pollution. We have, however, attempted to explore two aspects of the problem which seem often to be unduly neglected in many discussions of pollution control — the need for substantial uniformity in nationwide control policies (or offsetting fiscal transfers) in view of the interjurisdictional competition for industrial tax base, and the apparent necessity, more on political rather than economic grounds, of providing some transitional subsidization to existing plants in order to facilitate their conversion to the new order. Without easing the pain of adjustment for both regions and industries in some way, we would argue it is unlikely that rigorous pollution standards (or high enough prices) can in fact politically be set and enforced. The course of most existing legislation in both Canada and the United States provides some support for this view. If this argument is correct, the main points which ought to be kept in mind in designing any subsidy program are, as we have shown, four: (1) it should be transitional; (2) it should be open, i.e., its beneficiaries should be well publicized;(3) it should be as technologically unbiased as possible; and (4) it should be backed by a credible threat of strict enforcement after the transitional period. These and most of the other points on fiscal measures in the present paper, then, should be viewed as supplements to, rather than replacements for, the conventional economists' recommendations for "pricing" pollution.

We hope that those who read this paper will not be exasperated by our seeming contradiction — pollutors alone should pay to repair their damages but we all should assist in the short run. As economists we see the objectivity of imposing costs only on those who pollute; as realists and pollutors we are not so naive as to hope for the immediate introduction of a new pricing system for our environmental factors, without the offering of a carrot or two. This paper is the product of our realist frame of mind: given that some assistance is necessary, how can this aid be minimal, non-distorting, and temporary? We hope our discussion assists in making realists out of the economists, and economists out of the realists.

1   An interesting question, which we make no attempt to answer, is whether there is in fact more pollution in Canada in the 1970s than in Britain in the 1850s or in India today or whether we are just more aware of it.
2   For useful general discussions of these broader issues, see A.V. Kneese and B.T. Bower, *Managing Water Quality: Economics, Technology, Institutions* (Baltimore: John Hopkins Press, 1968); A. Devos, ed., *The Pollution Reader* (Montreal: Harvest House, 1968); and Leonard Waverman, "Pollution: A Problem in Economics," in L.H. Officer and L.B. Smith, eds., *Canadian Economic Problems and Policies* (Toronto: McGraw-Hill, 1970), pp. 318-34.
3   The suggestive analysis of a "market" solution to pollution problems put forward by J.H. Dales, *Pollution, Property and Prices* (Toronto: University of Toronto Press, 1968) is not discussed here. For discussion of Dales's proposal, see Waverman, "Pollution," pp. 331-3, and Richard W. Judy, "Economic Incentives and Environmental Control," paper presented to the International Symposium on Environmental Disruption in the Modern World, Tokyo, March 1970.
4   The truth in the sense of what they would pay to acquire their share of a collective good. See James M. Buchanan, *The Supply and Demand of Public Goods* (Chicago: Rand McNally, 1968) for a thorough discussion of the problems of providing collective goods.
5   A great deal of pollution is, of course, due to inadequate treatment of municipal sewage: cities as large as Halifax and Quebec do not have any primary treatment of sewage, while only Toronto among major Canadian cities has 100 per cent primary treatment.
6   It should be noted that the present discussion does not take into account the apocalyptic, but unfortunately often well-reasoned, forecasts of the extinc-

tion of life on "spaceship Earth" as a result of our environmental tampering. These fears appear to be concerned much more with air than water pollution and cannot be evaluated in economic terms anyway: if there is a finite probability that we are all going to kill ourselves soon through some particular action, there is indeed an infinite social cost involved, and immediate and complete prohibition of the "bad" is the only possible solution, whatever the cost to anyone in terms of reduced comfort. We are concerned here, however, not with such cataclysmic possibilities but with the much broader and milder range of economic problems involved in the usual water pollution situation.

7   As noted earlier, we do not discuss here the incidence of the costs and benefits from either pollution or its abatement, but it should be noted that there may certainly be interjurisdictional exporting and importing of these costs and benefits through trade patterns in "pollution-intensive" products. These effects, as well as those on the geographical location of production processes which produce both bads and goods (referred to below), can be more rigorously analysed conceptually through a model such as that developed in Charles E. McClure, Jr., "Taxation, Substitution, and Industrial Location," *Journal of Political Economy, LXXVIII* (January-February 1970), pp. 112-32, although there are as yet few data which would enable us to apply this analysis in practice.

8   The federal government might also try to induce – it cannot compel – a little more rationality in the organization of service areas by extra incentives to co-operative efforts and the like, though any such incentives are unlikely to be substantial enough to make much difference. Technical and economic arguments suggest that these service districts and the related aid should be functional (single-purpose) in character, although political considerations usually suggest broader aid to existing local governments, or at least channelling any assistance through them. No doubt this process would be somewhat inefficient in terms of the effects on the desired objective (water quality), but some inefficiency is the price that one pays for decentralization; any offsetting benefits do not, of course, show up in the usual economic calculation.

9   The US Department of the Interior has calculated that the capital outlay required to obtain adequate water standards (at least 85 per cent reduction of BOD and of settleable and suspended solids) by 1973 will be approximately $8 billion dollars for urban areas and between $2.6 and $4.6 billion dollars for industry. Federal Water Pollution Control Administration, *The Costs of Clean Water* (Washington, DC, 1968).

10 One of the services offered by the Ontario Water Resources Commission is that the agency will construct the necessary facilities and lease them to the municipality. The lease charge is sufficient to amortize the agencies' investment in twenty-five to thirty years.

11 Indeed, in one US government publication a few years ago, such measures were seen to be the main solution to the problem of financing local sewage treatment facilities. Public Health Service, *Problems in Financing Sewage Treatment Facilities* (Washington, DC, 1962).

12 The average (mean) sized project was therefore just under $200,000 and the mean loan to a municipality was approximately $3,000,000. Since 25 per cent of the loan was forgiven if the project was completed by an agreed date, this amount includes a grant element (assuming all projects to have finished on time) of $68,000,000, or roughly $50,000 per project and $750,000 per municipality.

13 The actual loans were $1.2 billion, but it appears from 1956-64 data that perhaps one-third of this amount was for water supply and purification projects. See J.A. Vance, K.B. Symous, and D.A. McTavish, "The Diverse Effects of Water Pollution on the Economy of Domestic and Municipal Water Use," Background Paper A4-1-5, Canadian Council of Resource Ministers, 1966.

14 Some grant programs seem unnecessarily perverse in their distributive effects, however. In 1969, for example, the Ontario Water Resources Commission began to lend money to municipalities where the expected per capita costs of constructing and operating sewage plants is well above the provincial average of $120. The program is expected to continue until 1976 at a total cost of some $80 million. The areas thus subsidized are largely in recreational areas. For example, the subsidy to Port Carling will be $135 per capita and in Haliburton $150 per capita. As the summer residents of these areas are hardly in the low income tail of the economy, this grant appears somewhat misguided.

15 The Ontario Development Corporation will begin in fiscal 1970-1 to lend money at favourable interest rates to "small" businesses for purposes of pollution abatement. The province has set aside $5 million for this program in 1970-1 (Ontario Budget Statement, 1970).

16 See, especially, Kneese and Bower, *Managing Water Quality*.

17 The Canada Water Act will apparently establish an effluent charge system, which is in accordance with most expert thinking on this subject. But the government's rather laboured argument against the "licence to pollute" view, that these fees are justified because they are earmarked to construct plants or take other action to provide better water, completely misses the point. As has often been demonstrated, this use of funds may or may not be optimal, but it has nothing whatever to do with the appropriate level of charges – except that the more central treatment there is, the lower the charges should be. The real justification for this earmarking must therefore be the traditional political argument that it will make the new taxes more acceptable than they would otherwise be.

18 The great differences which some analysts (e.g., Judy, "Economic Incentives and Environmental Control") see between differential pollution standards and an effective system of effluent charges in terms of informational and political aspects seem overstated. There are indeed serious problems with both approaches, and it may well be the charging system has an advantage in these respects, but we really have no evidence one way or another on the probability of mis-specification for these reasons or on the sensitivity of the results to such mis-specification.

'Pulp and paper is concerned about water pollution'

Pulp and paper mills have undoubtedly been a major contributor to water pollution in some areas. This industry, however, is extremely important to the Canadian economy. In October of 1969, Mr Robert Schmon, president of the Ontario Paper Company, addressed the National Executives' Conference of Water Pollution Abatement in Washington. In his address, reprinted in part below, Mr Schmon outlines the methods his company is employing to combat pollution and the resources being devoted to the problem. Mr Schmon also has some interesting comments on the role of government in the fight against environmental pollution. It is also instructive to compare the views of a man who is primarily concerned about international competition, profits, and shareholders, with those of the academics in the previous selections.

... I will discuss some industry aspects of water pollution, but will speak primarily of the experience, policy and plans of my company, not just because I feel some competence in relating our story but because pollution is individual and specific. Each company within our industry, in fact each plant within a company, has its particular circumstances requiring its own technical and economic solutions.

My company is a subsidiary of the Tribune Company, a holding company which publishes the *Chicago Tribune, Chicago Today*, the *New York Daily News*, and five newspapers in Florida, notably the *Fort Lauderdale News* and the *Orlando Sentinel*. The Canadian operations, with which I am concerned, include the Ontario Paper Company Limited which operates a newsprint mill and by-products plants at Thorold, Ontario, and its subsidiary, Quebec North Shore Paper Company, which operates a larger newsprint mill at Baie Comeau, Quebec. Our combined annual capacity is 550,000 tons of newsprint, increasing next year to 750,000 tons when an expansion at the Baie Comeau mill is completed.

Like all pulp and paper mills, we require large quantities of water. Our two mills combined use close to 50 million gallons a day, about the same as a city of 300,000 people. We have two kinds of waste: suspended solids such as minute fibres and bark particles; and dissolved solids such as wood sugars, lignins, and cellulose organics. These wastes may adversely affect fish life and may present aesthetic problems but do not have the human health hazards of municipal waste.

The specific pollution problems in our two mills are poles apart. At Thorold we are in a highly industrialized and urbanized area. Our problem is compounded because our effluent flows through two communities with a total population of 115,000 on its way to a fresh water basin, Lake Ontario. At our Baie Comeau plant in the province of Quebec we are in a remote area on salt water where tides run as high as 16 to 17 feet. This is another complexity of our industry. One mill may be located in a major metropolitan area, another is far off, still others are in medium size communities in relatively well developed areas. So there is no panacea for water pollution. Solutions must be tailor-made for each mill. This means money, lots of it. It also means time to develop and put into effect the right treatment at the right place. In spite of many significant accomplishments there is still a long way to go and a lot to learn.

In Canada, it seems to me that until the 1930s the priority with industrial developers and government leaders on federal, provincial, and municipal levels was to encourage economic development and expansion without regard to the cumulative impact of pollution. No one, it seemed, considered that the vast natural wealth of our inland water system would be endangered by human interference. Perhaps there was a sense of false security because Canada has 9% of the total flow of all rivers in the world and only 1% of the population. The simple fact is that these vast water resources *are* endangered and something must be and is being done about it.

I want to emphasize strongly that *all* society has contributed to water pollution. *All* society has a responsibility to overcome it. No one in industry, government, or the public can afford to just point the finger at the other fellow. It is *everybody's* business.

The pulp and paper industry in Canada recognizes its responsibility and the need for a sustained program to reduce or eliminate harmful effects of its effluents on the environment. Detailed data compiled by co-operative task forces show that in the period 1960 through 1966, mills accounting for 75% of total Canadian production installed recovering facilities costing more than $64 million, appreciably reducing the pollution load. (This is about 5% of the total capital expenditure during that period.) I am not trying to make a case here that the industry has done everything it should, but what I am trying to say is that it has done a great deal more than it is given credit for.

In our own company we can date pollution abatement activities back to 1935 when we established our research department and stipulated that one of its prime objectives was to reduce pollution and waste by fostering development of profitable new products from our effluent. Since then we have spent more than $4 million in research and development on by-products alone. Our research expenditures have now accelerated and we are spending about 50% of the total research budget in the by-product and pollution abatement areas. We have spent or are committed to spend more than $16 million capital in waste utilization and removal. These are considerable sums to a Canadian company like ours with annual sales of a little over $100 million.

In 1943 we built the first commercially successful plant in North America producing ethyl alcohol from spent sulphite liquor. The process was an adaptation of previous European practices. This plant, still in operation, removes some 25 tons a day of sugars from our effluent. In 1952 we started our own patented process to make vanillin, a synthetic vanilla, which removes 25 tons of other organics. These two by-product operations, which constitute 8% of our gross sales, produce revenue. However, not everyone can make alcohol or vanillin. The markets are limited, but it is the route we chose. Perhaps we were fortunate . . .

But if I or anyone in our management today get too heady with these successes we remind ourselves that a few years ago we invested in an oxalic acid plant that ran into technical and market difficulties and we had to close it down this spring. Not everything works in this struggle. In addition, our vanillin plant, while reducing the biological oxygen demand of our waste, creates an aesthetic problem due to colour and foam. . . .

So be it for yesterday. Now we must move faster. The condition of our environment and the temper of our times impatiently demand action. Regulatory bodies, encouraged by public opinion, are pressing for water quality standards that will require considerable investment and effort on industry's part. Nonetheless the job must be done.

The exact cost faced by our industry is difficult to establish, in part through lack of uniformity in legislation across Canada and in part through the lack of proven technology in some aspects of pollution abatement. However, it is estimated that stream pollution abatement in Canada's paper industry could require more than $250 million in capital funds, with annual operating charges of some $40 million. This does not include prior treatment such as evaporation and burning which could add to these already high costs. Such expenditures could significantly weaken the Canadian industry's competitive position in world markets. Most of these expenditures will be for one purpose only – to maintain and improve the environment. They will not increase productivity and, in most cases, there will be no financial return.

Our own company has just announced at the Thorold mill a $5 million program over two years which we hope will get us to the point of removing at least 85% of both dissolved and suspended solids. We hope to accomplish this through external treatment for suspended solids and an evaporation and burning process for dissolved solids. We are researching a process to recover reusable chemicals to reduce operating costs of this program to a break-even point. To approach this, at least an additional $3 million will be involved, and we will be lucky to achieve this objective. The risk is increased operating costs anywhere up to $5.00 per ton.

Any further improvement from this point, will very sharply increase our costs. To use the words of one of our experts – "the leaner the effluent, the fatter the bill." So we are faced with the delicate task of meeting exacting current and future standards in a time of relentlessly rising costs while still keeping our business on a sound economic basis not only for our shareholders, but for our customers, employees, suppliers, and the communities in which we live.

I do not regard this as all bad news. The pressures being exerted on us will force us to improve our technology, continuing the search for new by-products, recoverable chemicals, and tighter in-plant measures. But I suggest the industry must look beyond that to major break-throughs in pulping and paper-making techniques that will minimize pollution by reducing effluents, and by finding profitable uses for the effluents that are produced.

However, that may be papermaking in the 21st century. It does not negate the fact that we are facing the problem now, recognizing that some of the large investment we have in plant and equipment may have to be scrapped or changed radically.

The pulp and paper industry occupies a position of considerable importance in Canada's economy. It accounts for 1/7 of Canada's total exports and is one of the country's leading employers. Its growth and position as a major provider of employment and foreign exchange would be impaired if it must face alone the tremendous cost burden of pollution abatement. We have been advised by federal and provincial government representatives that anti-pollution measures should be included as part of production costs, and I presume they mean passed on to the customer. Looking at it realistically, we are not going to be able to pass on all these costs. It is for this reason that I, along with my colleagues in the industry, seek assistance from the three levels of government in Canada.

There are several ways in which we think the governments could legitimately and justifiably provide incentives. I refer specifically to such items as sales taxes on equipment used in pollution abatement.

Why should we pay these? Why should municipalities increase our property and building evaluations when we are spending money for public benefit? We could be greatly assisted if the federal government would improve recovery of expenditure through more advantageous depreciation rates and make funds available at low interest rates to industries undertaking approved abatement programs.

Lastly, I would caution against pushing industry into unnecessary expenditures in the understandable haste to control pollution. I have already indicated the differences between our own problems in our two locations. In one — as with other mills in remote areas — we can install satisfactory pollution controls at substantially less cost. What I am suggesting is that the different situations facing each plant should be recognized and that blanket and inflexible directives and regulations should not be imposed. It would be illogical to insist on treatment just for treatment's sake.

I am particularly aware of this because at the moment the regulatory situation in Canada is under review. Each province has its own regulatory body but the federal government is presenting to the current session of Parliament a new Canada Water Act designed to give common policy across the country. The Act advocates, among other things, regional boards with representatives from government and industry. I think this is a useful step, not only to provide a much-needed exchange of technical and research data, but to permit examination of all sides of the problem, to establish realistic and attainable timetables, and to develop co-operative information programs to acquaint the public with what is being done.

I emphasize that this last point is one of the chief problems. It is unfortunate that the good deeds of industry do not get equal publicity with the bad. A company can announce a major pollution control undertaking and the story is tucked away on a back page. On the other hand if a company is notified to improve its program or is fined for not doing enough, that news lands on page one and the adverse reaction of the public is reflected on industry generally. For the man in the street, it is often difficult to realize that something has been done and is being done because there is a sizable time lag not only through the research stage but in the actual implementation. In the program we announced last month at Thorold, it will be two years before the public will see any obvious effect. I am sure that in the next two years we are going to receive a lot of adverse comment despite our program and the announcements we have made about it.

So money and technology are not enough. There must also be understanding. Without it we cannot marshall the full force of our society to control water pollution. That is the essential point I want to make. The public is concerned. The government is concerned. I can assure you that my company and the Canadian pulp and paper industry are concerned. Let us now try to understand each other's problems and desires so that we may move together more effectively toward environmental improvements that will provide conditions for healthful and pleasant living which all of us have every right to expect and enjoy.

Part 4

Broader conceptual approaches

The problem of social cost

The concluding two selections describe different conceptual approaches to the pollution problem. "If factors of production are thought of as rights," states the author of the first selection, "it becomes easier to understand that the right to do something which has a harmful effect is also a factor of production." Professor R.H. Coase's article appeared in the October 1960 issue of the *Journal of Law and Economics.* His approach to the problem is still a subject of discussion in the economic literature.

THE PROBLEM TO BE EXAMINED

This paper is concerned with those actions of business firms which have harmful effects on others. The standard example is that of a factory the smoke from which has harmful effects on those occupying neighbouring properties. The economic analysis of such a situation has usually proceeded in terms of a divergence between the private and social product of the factory, in which economists have largely followed the treatment of Pigou in *The Economics of Welfare*. The conclusions to which this kind of analysis seems to have led most economists is that it would be desirable to make the owner of the factory liable for the damage caused to those injured by the smoke, or alternatively, to place a tax on the factory owner varying with the amount of smoke produced and equivalent in money terms to the damage it would cause, or finally, to exclude the factory from residential districts (and presumably from other areas in which the emission of smoke would have harmful effects on others). It is my contention that the suggested courses of action are inappropriate, in that they lead to results which are not necessarily, or even usually, desirable.

THE RECIPROCAL NATURE OF THE PROBLEM

The traditional approach has tended to obscure the nature of the choice that has to be made. The question is commonly thought of as one in which A inflicts harm on B and what has to be decided is: how should we restrain A? But this is wrong. We are dealing with a problem of a reciprocal nature. To avoid the harm to B would inflict harm on A. The real question that has to be decided is: should A be allowed to harm B or should B be allowed to harm A? The problem is to avoid the more serious harm. I instanced in my previous article[1] the case of a confectioner the noise and vibrations from whose manchinery disturbed a doctor in his work. To avoid harming the doctor would inflict harm on the confectioner. The problem posed by this case was essentially whether it was worth while, as a result of restricting the methods of production which could be used by the confectioner, to secure more doctoring at the cost of a reduced supply of confectionery products. Another example is afforded by the problem of straying cattle which destroy crops on neighbouring land. If it is inevitable that some cattle will stray, an increase in the supply of meat can only be obtained at the expense of a decrease in the supply of crops. The nature of the choice is clear: meat or crops. What answer should be given is, of course, not clear unless we know the value of what is obtained as well as the value of what is sacrificed to obtain it. To give another example, Professor George J. Stigler instances the contamination of a stream.[2] If we assume that the harmful effect of the pollution is that it kills the fish, the question to be decided is: is the value of the fish lost greater or less than the value of the product which the contamination of the stream makes possible. It goes almost without saying that this problem has to be looked at in total *and* at the margin . . .

I need not devote much space to discussing the similar error involved in the suggestion that smoke producing factories should, by means of zoning regulations, be removed from the districts in which the smoke causes harmful effects. When the change in the location of the factory results in a reduction in production, this obviously needs to be taken into account and weighed against the harm which would result from the factory remaining in that location. The aim of such regulation should not be to eliminate smoke pollution but rather to secure the optimum amount of smoke pollution, this being the amount which will maximise the value of production.

A CHANGE OF APPROACH

It is my belief that the failure of economists to reach correct conclusions about the treatment of harmful effects cannot be ascribed simply to a few slips in analysis. It stems from basic defects in the current approach to problems of welfare economics. What is needed is a change of approach.

Analysis in terms of divergencies between private and social products concentrates attention on particular deficiencies in the system and tends to nourish the belief that any measure which will remove the deficiency is necessarily desirable. It diverts attention from those other changes in the system which are inevitably associated with the corrective measure, changes which may well produce more harm than the original deficiency . . . But it is not necessary to approach the problem in this way. Economists who study problems of the firm habitually use an opportunity cost approach and compare the receipts obtained from a given combination of factors with alternative business arrangements. It would seem desirable to use a similar approach when dealing with questions of economic policy and to compare the total product yielded by alternative social arrangements . . . But it is of course, desirable that the choice between different social arrangements for the solution of economic problems should be carried out in broader terms than this and that the total effect of these arrangements in all spheres of life should be taken into account. As Frank H. Knight has so often emphasized, problems of welfare economics must ultimately dissolve into a study of aesthetics and morals.

A second feature of the usual treatment of the problems discussed in this article is that the analysis proceeds in terms of a comparison between a state of laissez-faire and some kind of ideal world. This approach inevitably leads to a looseness of thought since the nature of the alternatives being compared is never clear. In a state of laissez-faire, is there a monetary, a legal or a political system and if so, what are they? In an ideal world, would there be a monetary, a legal or a political system and if so, what would they be? The answers to all these questions are shrouded in mystery and every man is free to draw whatever conclusions he likes. Actually very little analysis is required to show that an ideal world is better than a state of laissez-faire, unless definitions of a state of laissez faire and an ideal world happen to be the same. But the whole discussion is largely irrelevant for questions of economic policy since whatever we may have in mind as our ideal world, it is clear that we have not yet discovered how to get to it from where we are. A better approach would seem to be to start our analysis with a situation approximating that which actually exists, to examine the effects of a proposed policy change and to attempt to decide whether the new situation would be, in total, better or worse than the original one. In this way, conclusions for policy would have some relevance to the actual situation.

A final reason for the failure to develop a theory adequate to handle the problem of harmful effects stems from a faulty concept of a factor of production. This is usually thought of as a physical entity which the businessman acquires and uses (an acre of land, a ton of fertiliser) instead of as a right to perform certain (physical) actions. We may speak of a person owning land and using it as a factor of production but what the land-owner in fact possesses is the right to carry out a circumscribed list of actions. The rights of a land-owner are not unlimited. It is not even always possible for him to remove the land to another place, for instance, by quarrying it. And although it may be possible for him to exclude some people from using "his" land, this may not be true of others. For example, some people may have the right to cross the land. Furthermore, it may or may not be possible to erect certain types of buildings or to grow certain crops or to use particular drainage systems on the land. This does not come about simply because of government regulation. It would be equally true under the common law. In fact it would be true under any system of law. A system in which the rights of individuals were unlimited would be one in which there were no rights to acquire.

If factors of production are thought of as rights, it becomes easier to understand that the right to do something which has a harmful effect (such as the creation of smoke, noise, smells, etc.) is also a factor of production. Just as we may use a piece of land in such a way as to prevent someone else from crossing it, or parking his car, or building his house upon it, so we may use it in such a way as to deny him a view or quiet or unpolluted air. The cost of exercising a right (of using a factor of production) is always the loss which is suffered elsewhere in consequence of the exercise of that right — the inability to cross land, to park a car, to build a house, to enjoy a view, to have peace and quiet or to breathe clean air.

It would clearly be desirable if the only actions performed were those in which what was gained was worth more than what was lost. But in choosing between social arrangements within the context of which individual decisions are made, we have to bear in mind that a change in the existing system which will lead to an improvement in some decisions may well lead to a worsening of others. Furthermore we have to take into account the costs involved in operating the various social arrangements (whether it be the working of a market or of a government department), as well as the costs involved in moving to a new system. In devising and choosing between social arrangements we should have regard for the total effect. This, above all, is the change in approach which I am advocating.

1 "The Federal Communications Commission," *Journal of Law and Economics, II* (1959).
2 G.J. Stigler, *The Theory of Price* (New York: Macmillan, 1947).

The pollution problem

"No man can arrogate to himself the right to alter the common environment. Such acts must be subject to public regulation and control . . ." The author of that quotation and the following selection is Director of the Canadian Council of Resource Ministers, Christian de Laet. He places heavy emphasis on the resources management approach to environmental pollution as the long-run solution to the problem. Mr de Laet also discusses the social aspects of pollution and the inability of man, as shown in the past, to foresee the consequences of his present actions.

We are living today in a paradoxical situation; as the quantity of our usable air, water and soil declines, the demand for it increases. As this happens, we become more and more concerned with the quality of the air, water and soil which is left.

Few would say we should ignore pollution and its attendant problems. But what is to be done about it?

We are all familiar with reports of malodorous rivers, unpotable water, poisoned, unyielding earth and noxious clouds of lung-searing air blanketing our cities and choking their inhabitants. Such graphic descriptions are depressingly familiar and seldom accurate.

There is no immediate shortage of basic resources in Canada, and none is in view. However, this does not mean that we should ignore the prospect of such calamities. Contamination of the soil is a factor which at worst interferes with the livelihood of but a very small section of our population. Air pollution has not reached critically intolerable levels anywhere in Canada and to a large extent water is still of a reasonable quality. We are tackling problems of environmental management although we may not be doing so on the scale we would all wish. It is not a matter of damping down the vivid fires of alarm lit by the most pessimistic; neither is it useful to develop cliff-hanging crisis responses where no crisis exists.

Until recently, Canada was a land where unprincipled over-exploitation of our resources was a patent of virtue. Since the turn of the century, the necessity of developing secondary industries and the attendant problem of social and economic development inevitably created a need for responsible planning. A cowboy type attitude towards unlimited spaces, glorifying consumption rather than capital formation or the conservation of our heritage, is slowly giving way to a spaceship type attitude with "recycle" and "reuse" the keywords. There is nothing new to a wise approach to managing our environment. It is just a matter of increasing our diligence to face problems which may otherwise accelerate out of reach.

To alter our environment is to alter an enduring pattern of survival. All life is based on carbon, oxygen, nitrogen and hydrogen, and our contacts with these occur through the basic resources of air, water and soil. These basic resources must be free to complete their respective cycles relatively intact. If they are impaired or altered in any significant way, the basis for survival takes on a new configuration with a spread far exceeding man's ability to evolve or adapt.

Although man is unique in his ability to alter the environment, he is also unique in his ability to create an imbalance in the existing environment. This alteration undertaken individually or collectively to produce more satisfactory surroundings or greater social and economic returns, creates a man-influenced environment to the point where there is no limit, except perhaps his own physical limitations, to what man can do to it.

The addition of external material that does not occur in the system also causes imbalances. In this case, the system generally cannot absorb and integrate the foreign matter, and there is an impairment of efficiency, if not the formation of new products, resulting in spectacular and sudden effects.

We might define pollution as the addition to a balanced environmental system of a quantity of external matter greater than the system can safely absorb over a stated period of time, resulting in partial or total destruction of the system. Whichever way we choose to call the imbalance in the relationship between man and his environment, the condition stems from the crowding of time and space in our response to social and economic pressures.

Manufacturing, especially when it involves inorganic materials, creates by-products that are not easily integrated into the natural cycles of our environment. But as these are often products of little commercial value, they cannot be sold and must be otherwise disposed of. To dispose of them on land is expensive as land must be bought or rented. Sometimes this is necessary. But water and air are free, and wherever possible industries use these reservoirs for disposing of their wastes.

Industrialization and urbanization have drawn the population away from agriculture and into large urban concentrations. Large concentrations of people and industry produce large concentrations of waste material. This is a relatively new development in the history of mankind, and we haven't yet learned how to deal with it.

Two other factors compound our difficulties. One is that in a densely populated area many people and interests want to use the same resource for different and conflicting purposes. This has created the concept of a multi-use resource, requiring arbitration between users of varying importance to the local, regional, and national economies, and affecting interests and life forms of varying vulnerabilities. We discover that air, water and soil, as related to local situations, are not unlimited after all.

The second area of difficulty arises because the vehicles of air and water that we use for waste disposal are uncontained, and drift freely beyond the man-made environment that charged them with wastes to invade the surrounding countryside and communities.

The city is out of balance with its surroundings. It is on its way to destroying itself as a viable environment for mankind. Its own wastes accumulate in and around it, polluting its water supply and charging its air with noxious materials. It renders its surroundings unsuitable for recreation, for habitation, and possibly even for industrialization. Man as the maker of his environment, and man as the product of his environment, are engaged in a conflict that could become deadly.

What should we do? To my mind the key to beginning to solve this potentially nightmarish situation is to instill a concept of individual responsibility: pollution is primarily a social problem.

Society imposes constraints of many kinds on individual behavior as it affects the common good. The individual voluntarily accepts certain codes of behavior, based on an understanding of benefits and penalties to his physical, social and economic well-being. What we understand is what affects us directly, and we actively support measures that promote our direct interests. But what is not immediate and does not confront us directly, individually, and unequivocally, we tend to overlook and relegate responsibility elsewhere.

Pollution does not seem to affect us in our daily routine. We place our garbage in neat containers and a truck takes it away. Our drainage and sewage disappears mysteriously into a municipal sewage system and we forget it. We turn on our faucets and obtain reasonably clean water. Foods and amenities are available to us.

Our laissez-faire attitude carries over into the corporate world. Both industries and municipalities are often unconcerned with the effects of discharge once they depart the immediate vicinity. The claim is also made that the benefits they bestow on the community far outweigh the disadvantages.

Man has never been noted for taking the long look, for building for future generations. Individual man is often too unsettled and rootless to allow even a selfish view of heritage. We are perhaps too optimistic in our belief in the manifest destiny of modern technology.

All problems are not necessarily susceptible to merely technical attack. Our attitudes to pollution must change. The cost of control increases from day to day, and some aspects cannot be reversed, no matter what effort we apply.

Absolute levels of pollution can be defined. However, these levels may be above or below the tolerance levels in a specific problem area. Tolerance to a given level of pollution is dependent on the local resource concentration, on the local uses to which the resource is put, and on the aesthetic and social standards of the community.

It is becoming increasingly clear that man's presence on earth, in ever growing numbers is largely subject to the amount of pollution that the natural environment can stand. With the exception of war, this is the greatest threat to our continued existence. On the other hand, it would be unrealistic to think that pollution could be wiped out entirely, for it seems to be a condition of the human presence. As man today sometimes appears to be on the brink of self-destruction by war, so he is attacking himself on another level, by exceeding the ability of his natural environment to cope with his increasing numbers and activities. We acknowledge the existence of a natural environmental order which, when upset, tends to destroy. We know further that the basic elements of air, earth and water are fundamental to man's survival. Yet until recently these concepts were seen and understood only abstractly, and the result was a "non-attitude" to the natural environment.

This situation is accented by the fact that in Canada, many regions are scarcely out of the settlement stage. Many people still tend to behave in terms of the free access to land, air and water enjoyed by the pastoral society. This becomes inoperative or at best a cause of friction when people congregate in increasingly large groups. More than 70 percent of Canadians now live in communities exceeding 2,000 persons. Because of this situation financing at the local level becomes a serious problem since there is a reluctance to pay any price for what is assumed to be a part of nature's boundless generosity.

These are merely symptoms of the environmental malaise produced by the fact that man often scarcely relates at all to his natural surroundings. Our social and technological advances, coupled with the move from a pastoral to an urban life, have encouraged the illusion that man has triumphed over nature and manufactured an environment of his own, independent of the elemental forces.

Until man began to transform his environment on a massive scale, and with it the environment of many other forms of life, the various interrelated and interdependent ecosystems that constitute the living world changed fairly gradually, without violent upheavals and dislocations.

With man's modern interventions, the rate and scale of environmental change have increased drastically, destroying the balance among existing ecosystems to an unprecedented degree and with unpredictable consequences. This situation raises questions about the purpose and nature of man's transformation of the natural environment.

There are, and can be, no moral guidelines to determine how man should act in relation to his environment. The law of evolution, which is the law of the jungle, decrees that the dominant species at a given time and place has no restrictions on its freedom of action other than its physical limitations. Its future and fate are very much in its own hands.

The only criterion for environmental management is our own welfare, our survival and continued evolutionary progress. Assuming that we know what is good for us, we should shape our environment accordingly.

The problem consists of this: that we do not know how to achieve the kind of environment we want, and that we do not know what may be the side effects and by-products in one area of our environment by our interventions in another area. Thus, our attempts at environmental control and transformation are often self-defeating, with unforeseen difficulties that exceed the benefits obtained.

Man should be able to define in general terms the kind of environment he would like to create for himself, and the consequent modifications of the natural environment. For example, we want to satisfy our physical needs by converting natural resources to our uses. We also have social and physiological needs such as recreation, relaxation and contact with nature which are intimately dependent on our natural environment. Finally, we have intellectual and spiritual needs.

But we are hindered in defining our ideal environment with precision by the fact that natural resources are limited, and the satisfaction of all our needs makes conflicting demands upon our surroundings. We have so far been unable to reconcile the competing demands we make on our resources with the result that an advance in one field often entails a retrogression in another. We must establish our priorities and goals more clearly before we can manage our environment to the relative satisfaction of all.

From man's point of view, the conversion of natural resources to his own ends is the basic economic operation. This operation, which we may call exploitation of our environment, must be as efficient as possible. Resource conversion produces unusable by-products or waste materials which, if allowed to accumulate in the environment, will eventually render its exploitation less and less efficient. Concentrations of waste in the environment, especially in soil, become environmental pollution when they cause a discernible inefficiency in the exploitation of the environment.

In this sense, environmental pollution results from inefficient exploitation, or simply from bad environmental management. It represents, by definition, a net disservice to a given society or region. Therefore, in global terms, the elimination of environmental pollution will result in a net benefit to society. To state the proposition positively, we need more rational and efficient environmental management.

What we are really interested in is improving the management of our environment in terms of human ends. To talk about pollution control instead of environmental management is a negative and incomplete statement of the problem. Some may say that this is an unjustified distortion of the real issue, that it will confuse rather than clarify matters. Is this approach to environmental management a legitimate one?

The problems of improving environmental management are not so much technological as social. Essentially, they are problems of communication and education. It is axiomatic that before an educational program can be effective, the interest of those to whom it is directed must be aroused.

Public interest in pollution is undeniably high. It is higher than it will ever be in environmental management. The average citizen is not interested in theories of environmental management beyond the occasional lip-service to conservation. But he does become concerned and moved to action if his water tastes bad or is discolored, if his air is smog-filled, if his countryside is disfigured. However, it is always the "other" who pollutes. Those in a position to improve our environmental management will not act without the support of the people, the media and the politicians. If this support can only be generated and polarized by an essentially negative approach to the issue, no matter. In this case, as in many others, the end justifies the means. It is not only legitimate but necessary to appeal to whatever aspect of the human character will produce results. Put bluntly, an appeal to self-interest is always more productive than an appeal to the common interest.

As public perception of the problem of environmental management tends to focus on the negative aspects — on the failures, the breakdowns, and their consequent drawbacks — attempts to generate support for improved environmental management must be based on the elimination of these drawbacks. Information programs, propaganda, motivational and educational programs must appeal to the self-interest of resource users.

Western society has a strong tradition of private ownership of land and even, up to a point, of water. In general, people are most responsive to an appeal to conserve and protect their own private property, and least responsive to an appeal to protect common property.

There is also a strong tradition of individual responsibility for actions traceable to the individual in our Judeo-Christian mores. Therefore, appeals for public action should be based as far as possible on these twin principles — individual (or corporate) responsibility for waste products, and the importance of one man's activities not infringing the property rights of others. At the same time, the rights of ownership are not absolute. We must emphasize the doctrines of public nuisance and *abus de droit*. We should appeal to general or social or common responsibility for pollution control only where it is impossible to pinpoint individual responsibility. Surprisingly, everyone's conception of dominant use of a resource is influenced by his "own need."

Inevitably, individual interests conflict as we are competing for limited resources. It may be in the interest of the chemical manufacturer to dump his wastes or to sell more pesticides, but not in the interest of the fisherman or the agriculturist. In this case we must appeal to the superordinate goal. Both are interested in the quality of their environment, and in having both water and chemical products.

No man can arrogate to himself the right to alter the common environment. Such acts must be subject to public regulation and control, and if their consequences are uncertain, as is often the case, they should be approached tentatively, experimentally, and incrementally.

It is essential to look at man and his world in an evolutionary perspective. We are not foreign to, or separate from, a so-called natural environment. We are simply one component, albeit the dominant one, of the present terrestrial environment. As such, there are no constraints — moral, philosophical or otherwise — except purely physical ones, on our freedom to manage our environment for our own ends. But this freedom to progress is also a freedom to retrogress. We have the opportunity and ability to achieve unparalleled quality of environment and human life, or to utterly destroy both.

We do not consciously desire the deterioration of our environment, yet we often cause it. This is due in part to lack of knowledge, to an inability to foresee the consequences of our acts, and in part to a lack of individual responsibility for these consequences, especially where common or public resources are concerned, and to a failure to understand and respect the common interests and rights of other men. We have an individual responsibility not to despoil the common environment, and a common responsibility not to mismanage our private property.

In persuading men to take account of the public good in their private actions, we must seek to demonstrate that the public interests and the private interest are in the long run identical.

Part 5

Appendices

Appendices

One question that is frequently asked about our pollution abatement is what provincial and federal legislation is being enacted to improve the environment. The following appendices contain the text of two recent pieces of legislation – one federal and one provincial – which deal respectively with water and air pollution. Anyone interested in environmental policy should be aware of what governments are trying to do, how they plan to achieve their objectives, and what economic costs may be incurred in executing these policies. The Canada Water Act was passed in 1970, giving the federal government the power to prohibit pollution of waterways and providing authority to act in cases of violation of the law. Appendix 2 includes the Ontario Air Pollution Control Act of 1967 and three regulations subsequently made under the Act.

1.   The Canada Water Act

AN ACT to provide for the management of the water resources of
Canada including research and the planning and implementation of
programs relating to the conservation, development and utilization
of water resources

[1969-70, c. 52]

WHEREAS the demands on the water resources of Canada are
increasing rapidly and more knowledge is needed of the nature,
extent and distribution of those resources, of the present and future
demands thereon and of the means by which those demands may be
met;

AND WHEREAS pollution of the water resources of Canada is a
significant and rapidly increasing threat to the health, well-being and
prosperity of the people of Canada and to the quality of the
Canadian environment at large and as a result it has become a matter
of urgent national concern that measures be taken to provide for
water quality management in those areas of Canada most critically
affected;

AND WHEREAS The Parliament of Canada is desirous that, in
addition, comprehensive programs be undertaken by the Government of Canada and by the Government of Canada in cooperation
with provincial governments, in accordance with the responsibilities
of the federal government and each of the provincial governments in
relation to water resources, for research and planning with respect to
those resources and for their conservation, development and
utilization to ensure their optimum use for the benefit of all
Canadians;

NOW, THEREFORE, Her Majesty, by and with the advice and consent
of the Senate and House of Commons of Canada, enacts as follows:

SHORT TITLE
1.   This Act may be cited as the *Canada Water Act*.

INTERPRETATION
2.   (1) In this Act
   "agency" means a water quality management agency the incorpora-

tion of which is procured or that is named pursuant to section 9 or 11;

"analyst" means an analyst designated pursuant to section 23;

"boundary waters" means the waters from main shore to main shore of the lakes and rivers and connecting waterways, or the portions thereof, along which the international boundary between the United States and Canada passes, including all bays, arms and inlets thereof, but not including tributary waters which in their natural channels would flow into such lakes, rivers and waterways, or waters flowing from such lakes, rivers and waterways, or the waters of rivers flowing across the boundary;

"federal agency" means a water quality management agency the incorporation of which is procured or that is named pursuant to section 11;

"federal waters" means waters under the exclusive legislative jurisdiction of the Parliament of Canada;

"inspector" means an inspector designated pursuant to section 23;

"inter-jurisdictional waters" means any waters, whether international, boundary or otherwise, that, whether wholly situated in a province or not, significantly affect the quantity or quality of waters outside such province;

"international waters" means waters of rivers that flow across the international boundary between the United States and Canada;

"Minister" means the Minister of Energy, Mines and Resources;

"prescribed" means prescribed by regulation;

"waste" means any substance that, if added to any waters, would degrade or alter or form part of a process of degradation or alteration of the quality of those waters to an extent that is detrimental to their use by man or by any animal, fish or plant that is useful to man, and includes any water that contains a substance in such a quantity or concentration, or that has been so treated, processed or changed, by heat or other means, from a natural state that it would, if added to any waters, degrade or alter or form part of a process of degradation or alteration of the quality of those waters to an extent that is detrimental to their use by man or by any animal, fish or plant that is useful to man;

"water quality management" means any aspect of water resource management that relates to restoring, maintaining or improving the quality of water;

"water resource management" means the conservation, development and utilization of water resources, and includes, with respect thereto, research, data collection and the maintaining of inventories, planning and the implementation of plans, and the control and regulation of water quantity and quality.

(2) Without limiting the generality of the definition of the term "waste" in this Act,

(a) any substance or any substance that is part of a class of substances prescribed pursuant to subparagraph 16(1)(a)(i),

(b) any water that contains any substance or any substance that is part of a class of substances in a quantity or concentration prescribed in respect of that substance or class of substances pursuant to subparagraph 16(1)(a)(iii),

shall, for the purposes of this Act, be deemed to be waste.

(3) This Act is binding on Her Majesty in right of Canada or a province and any agent thereof.

PART I
Comprehensive water resource management
Federal-provincial arrangements
3. For the purpose of facilitating the formulation of policies and programs with respect to the water resources of Canada and to ensure the optimum use of those resources for the benefit of all Canadians, having regard to the distinctive geography of Canada and the character of water as a natural resource, the Minister may, with the approval of the Governor in Council, enter into an arrangement with one or more provincial governments to establish, on a national, provincial, regional or lake or river-basin basis, intergovernmental committees or other bodies

(a) to maintain continuing consultation on water resource matters and to advise on priorities for research, planning, conservation, development and utilization relating thereto;

(b) to advise on the formulation of water policies and programs; and

(c) to facilitate the coordination and implementation of water policies and programs.

Comprehensive water resource management programs
4. Subject to this Act, the Minister may, with the approval of the

Governor in Council, with respect to any waters where there is a significant national interest in the water resource management thereof, from time to time enter into agreements with one or more provincial governments having an interest in the water resource management of those waters, providing for programs to

(*a*) establish and maintain an inventory of those waters,

(*b*) collect, process and provide data on the quality, quantity, distribution and use of those waters,

(*c*) conduct research in connection with any aspect of those waters or provide for the conduct of any such research by or in cooperation with any government, institution or person,

(*d*) formulate comprehensive water resource management plans, including detailed estimates of the cost of implementation of those plans and of revenues and other benefits likely to be realized from the implementation thereof, based upon an examination of the full range of reasonable alternatives and taking into account views expressed at public hearings and otherwise by persons likely to be affected by implementation of the plans,

(*e*) design projects for the efficient conservation, development and utilization of those waters, and

(*f*) implement any plans or projects referred to in paragraphs (*d*) and (*e*), and establishing or naming joint commissions, boards or other bodies empowered to direct, supervise and coordinate such programs.

5. (1) Subject to subsection (2), the Minister shall, with the approval of the Governor in Council, undertake directly,

(*a*) with respect to any federal waters, any program described in any of paragraphs 4(*a*) to (*e*) and the implementation of any program described in paragraph 4(*d*) or (*e*);

(*b*) with respect to any inter-jurisdictional waters where there is a significant national interest in the water resource management thereof, any program described in paragraph 4(*d*) or (*e*); and

(*c*) with respect to any international or boundary waters where there is a significant national interest in the water resource management thereof, any program described in paragraph 4(*d*) or (*e*) and the implementation of any such program.

(2) The Governor in Council shall not approve the undertaking by the Minister of any program pursuant to paragraph 1(*b*) or (*c*) unless he is satisfied that all reasonable efforts have been made by the Minister to reach an agreement under section 4 with the one or more provinial governments having an interest in the water resource management of the waters in question, and that those efforts have failed.

(3) In undertaking any programs pursuant to subsection (1), the Minister shall take into account any priorities for development recommended pursuant to paragraph 3(*a*).

6. The Minister may conduct research, collect data and establish inventories respecting any aspect of water resource management or the management of any specific water resources or provide for the conduct of any such research, data collection or inventory establishment by or in cooperation with any government, institution or person.

7. (1) Where, pursuant to section 4, the Minister enters into an agreement with one or more provincial governments, the agreement shall, where applicable, in respect of each program that is the subject of such agreement, specify

(*a*) the respective parts of the program to be undertaken by the Minister and the provincial government or governments that are parties to the agreement and the times at which and the manner in which such parts of the program are to be carried out;

(*b*) the proportions of the cost of the respective parts of the program that are to be paid by the Minister and the provincial government or governments and the times at which amounts representing such proportions are to be paid;

(*c*) the labour, land and materials that are to be supplied in relation to the respective parts of the program by the Minister and the provincial government or governments;

(*d*) the proportions in which any compensation awarded or agreed to be paid to any body or person suffering loss as a result of the program is to be paid by the Minister and the provincial government or governments;

(*e*) the amount of any loan or grant, constituting part or all of the cost of the program that is to be paid by the Minister, that is to be made or paid by the Minister to the provincial government or governments, and the manner in which the terms and conditions of the loan or grant are to be determined;

(*f*) the authority or authorities, whether an agent or agents of Her Majesty in right of Canada or a province or otherwise as may be agreed to be appropriate, that will be responsible for the under-taking, operation or maintenance of projects that form part of the program;

(*g*) the respective proportions of the revenues from the program that are to be paid to the Minister and the provincial government or governments; and

(*h*) the terms and conditions relating to the undertaking, operation and maintenance of the program.

(2) An agreement entered into pursuant to section 4 shall, where applicable, in respect of the joint commission, board or other body thereby established or named, provide for

(*a*) the constitution thereof, the members thereof that are to be appointed by the Minister and the provincial government or governments that are parties to the agreement and the terms and conditions of such appointments;

(*b*) the staff thereof that is to be supplied by the Minister and the provincial government or governments;

(*c*) the duties of the body and the powers that it may exercise in directing, supervising and coordinating the program;

(*d*) the keeping of accounts and records by the body;

(*e*) the annual submission by the body to the Minister and the provincial government or governments of operating and capital budgets in connection with the programs directed, supervised and coordinated by the body for the next following fiscal year for approval by the Governor in Council and such persons on behalf of the provincial government or governments as are designated in the agreement; and

(*f*) the submission by the body to the Minister and the provincial government or governments, within three months after the termi-nation of each fiscal year, of an annual report containing such information as is specified in the agreement.

PART II
Water quality management
Pollution of waters

8. Except in quantities and under conditions prescribed with respect to waste disposal in the water quality management area in question, including the payment of any effluent discharge fee prescribed therefor, no person shall deposit or permit the deposit of waste of any type in any waters comprising a water quality management area designated pursuant to section 9 or 11, or in any place under any conditions where such waste or any other waste that results from the deposit of such waste may enter any such waters.

Federal-provincial water quality management

9. In the case of

(*a*) any waters, other than federal waters, the water quality management of which has become a matter of urgent national concern, or

(*b*) any federal waters,

the Minister may, with the approval of the Governor in Council, from time to time enter into agreements with one or more provincial governments having an interest in the water quality management thereof, designating those waters as a water quality management area, providing for water quality management programs in respect thereof and authorizing the Minister, jointly with such one or more provincial governments, to procure the incorporation of a corporation without share capital, or to name an existing corporation that is an agent of Her Majesty in right of Canada or a province or that performs any function or duty on behalf of the Government of Canada or the government of a province, as a water quality management agency to plan, initiate and carry out, in conjunction with the Minister and such provincial government or governments, programs described in section 13 in respect of those waters.

10. (1) Where, pursuant to section 9, the Minister enters into an agreement with one or more provincial governments, the agreement shall, where applicable, in respect of each water quality management program that is the subject of such agreement, specify

(*a*) the responsibilities of the Minister and the provincial government or governments that are parties to the agreement and the times at which and the manner in which such responsibilities are to be undertaken;

(*b*) the proportions of the capital cost of the respective parts of the program that are to be paid by the Minister and the provincial government or governments and the times at which amounts representing such proportions are to be paid;

(*c*) the loans or contributions in respect of the cost of incorporation and operating expenses of the agency and the loan in respect of capital costs incurred by the agency that is to undertake the program, that are to be made or paid by the Minister and the provincial government or governments and the times at which such loans or contributions are to be made or paid;

(*d*) the labour, land and materials that are to be supplied by the Minister and the provincial government or governments to the agency that is to undertake the program;

(*e*) the proportions in which any compensation awarded or agreed to be paid to any body or person suffering loss as a result of the program is to be paid by the Minister and the provincial government or governments; and

(*f*) the terms and conditions relating to the undertaking, operation and maintenance of the program by the agency,

and each such agreement shall provide that it may be terminated, on six months written notice by any party to the agreement to all other parties thereto or on such lesser notice as may be agreed upon by all such parties, and that upon the expiration of the time fixed by such notice for the termination of the agreement any agency incorporated thereunder shall be wound up.

(2) An agreement entered into pursuant to section 9 shall, in respect of the agency the incorporation of which is thereby authorized to be procured, if any, provide for

(*a*) the proposed corporate name of the agency;

(*b*) the place within the water quality management area designated in the agreement where the head office of the agency is to be situated;

(*c*) the members thereof that are to be appointed by the Minister

and the provincial government or governments that are parties to the agreement and the terms and conditions of such appointments;
(*d*) the proposed by-laws of the agency; and
(*e*) the matters set out in paragraphs 7(2)(*b*) and 7(2)(*d*) to (*f*).

Federal water quality management
11. (1) Where, in the case of any interjurisdictional waters, the water quality management of those waters has become a matter of urgent national concern, and either
(*a*) the Governor in Council is satisfied that all reasonable efforts have been made by the Minister to reach an agreement under section 9 with the one or more provincial governments having an interest in the water quality management thereof, and that those efforts have failed, or
(*b*) although an agreement was reached under section 9 in respect thereof and an agency was incorporated or named thereunder, the Minister and the appropriate minister of each provincial government that was a party to the agreement disagreed with the recommendations of the agency with respect to water quality standards for those inter-jurisdictional waters and were unable to agree on a joint recommendation with respect thereto and as a result thereof the agreement under section 9 was terminated,
the Governor in Council may, on the recommendation of the Minister, designate such waters as a water quality management area and authorize the Minister to procure the incorporation of a corporation without share capital under Part II of the *Canada Corporations Act,* or to name an existing corporation that is an agent of Her Majesty in right of Canada or that performs any function or duty on behalf of the Government of Canada, as a water quality management agency to plan, initiate and carry out programs described in section 13 in respect of those waters.

(2) The Governor in Council may, on the recommendation of the Minister, designate any federal waters as a water quality management area and authorize the Minister to procure the incorporation of a corporation without share capital under Part II of the *Canada Corporations Act,* or to name an existing corporation that is an agent of Her Majesty in right of Canada or that performs any func-

tion or duty on behalf of the Government of Canada, as a water quality management agency to plan, initiate and carry out programs described in section 13 in respect of those waters.

(3) In procuring the incorporation of a federal agency pursuant to subsection (1) or (2), the Minister shall, with the approval of the Governor in Council, provide for
(*a*) the appointment of the members thereof by the Governor in Council for such terms and under such conditions as the Governor in Council deems suitable;
(*b*) the staff thereof that is to be supplied by the Minister; and
(*c*) the terms and conditions under which and the remuneration at which any staff may be appointed by the federal agency.

(4) The Minister may give directions to any federal agency with respect to the implementation of any water quality management program and, in so doing, he shall take into account any priorities for development recommended pursuant to paragraph 3(*a*).

12. (1) A federal agency is for all purposes an agent of Her Majesty and its powers may be exercised only as an agent of Her Majesty.

(2) A federal agency may, on behalf of Her Majesty, enter into contracts in the name of Her Majesty or in its name.

(3) Property acquired by a federal agency is the property of Her Majesty and title thereto may be vested in the name of Her Majesty or in its name.

(4) Actions, suits or other legal proceedings in respect of any right or obligation acquired or incurred by a federal agency on bahalf of Her Majesty, whether in its name or in the name of Her Majesty, may be brought or taken against that agency in the name of the agency in any court that would have jursidiction if it were not an agent of Her Majesty.

Water quality management agencies
13. (1) The objects of each water quality management agency shall be to plan, initiate and carry out programs to restore, preserve and enhance the water quality level in the water quality management

area for which the agency is incorporated or named and in carrying out those objects, subject to any agreement under section 9 relating to such water quality management area or to any direction of the Minister to a federal agency, the agency may, after taking into account views expressed to it, at public hearings and otherwise, by persons likely to have an interest therein, in respect of the waters comprising the water quality management area for which it is incorporated or named,

(*a*) ascertain the nature and quantity of waste present therein and the water quality level;

(*b*) undertake studies that enable forecasts to be made of the amounts and kinds of waste that are likely to be added to those waters in the future;

(*c*) develop and recommend to the Minister and, in the case of an agency other than a federal agency, to the appropriate minister of each provincial government that is a party to the agreement relating to the water quality management area, a water quality management plan including

(i) recommendations as to water quality standards for those waters or any part thereof and the times at which those standards should be attained,

(ii) recommendations, based upon the water quality standards recommended pursuant to subparagraph (i), as to the quantities and types of waste, if any, that may be deposited in those waters and the conditions under which any such waste may be deposited,

(iii) recommendations as to the treatment that may be required for any waste that is or may be deposited in those waters and the type of treatment facilities necessary to achieve the water quality standards recommended pursuant to subparagraph (i),

(iv) recommendations as to appropriate effluent discharge fees to be paid by persons for the deposit of waste in those waters and the time or times at which and the manner in which such fees should be paid,

(v) recommendations as to appropriate waste treatment and waste sample analysis charges to be levied by the agency for the treatment of waste at any waste treatment facility that is operated and maintained by it or for the analysis of any waste sample by it,

(vi) detailed estimates of the cost of implementation of the plan and of revenues and other benefits likely to be realized from the implementation thereof, and

(vii) estimates of the time within which the agency would become financially self-sustaining.

(2) Where an agency recommends a water quality management plan to the Minister, it shall forthwith cause the plan to be published in the *Canada Gazette* and shall publish a concise summary of the plan in a newspaper of general circulation in the area affected by the plan at least once a week for a period of four weeks; no such plan shall be approved until the expiration of seven clear days after the publication last so required.

(3) Where a water quality management plan recommended by an agency in respect of the waters comprising the water quality management area for which it is incorporated or named has been approved by the Minister and, in the case of an agency other than a federal agency, by the appropriate minister of each provincial government that is a party to the agreement relating to those waters, the agency may, in order to implement the water quality management plan,

(*a*) design, construct, operate and maintain waste treatment facilities and undertake the treatment of waste delivered to such facilities;

(*b*) undertake the collection of any charges prescribed for waste treatment at any waste treatment facility that is operated and maintained by it and for waste sample analysis carried out by it;

(*c*) undertake the collection of effluent discharge fees prescribed to be payable by any person for the deposit of waste in those waters;

(*d*) monitor, on a regular basis, water quality levels;

(*e*) provide facilities for the analysis of samples of waste and collect and provide data respecting the quantity and quality of waste and the effects thereof on those waters;

(*f*) regularly inspect any waste treatment facilities within the water quality management area for which it is incorporated or named, whether publicly or privately owned;

(g) publish or otherwise distribute such information as may be required under this Act; and

(h) do such other things as are necessary to achieve effective water quality management of those waters.

(4) Except with respect to loans authorized to be made by it by the Minister or a provincial government as described in paragraph 10(1)(c), an agency does not have power to borrow moneys, to issue securities or to guarantee the payment of any debt or obligation of any person.

14. (1) The members of an agency who are appointed by the Minister or by the Governor in Council and who are not employees in the public service of Canada shall be paid by the agency such remuneration as is authorized by the Governor in Council.

(2) The Minister may provide any agency with such officers and employees as may be necessary for the proper functioning of the agency, and may provide any such agency with such professional or technical assistance for temporary periods or for specific work as the agency may request.

(3) Subject to the agreement under which the incorporation of an agency was authorized to be procured or to any matter provided for under subsection 11(3) or any direction of the Minister under subsection 11(4) in respect of a federal agency, the agency may employ such officers and employees and such consultants and advisers as it considers necessary to enable it to carry out its objects and fix the terms and conditions of their employment and their remuneration, which shall be paid by the agency.

15. (1) Each agency shall maintain under the name of the agency, in a chartered bank, an account to which shall be deposited

(a) all amounts collected by the agency as or on account of charges levied for treatment of waste, the analysis of samples of waste or for the deposit of waste in the waters comprising the water quality management area for which the agency is incorporated or named, (*b*) contributions paid or loans made to the agency by the Government of Canada or the government of a province in respect of the cost of incorporation of the agency, in respect of its operating expenses or in respect of capital costs incurred by it, and

(*c*) interest received by the agency on securities purchased, acquired and held by it pursuant to subsection (2),

and out of which shall be paid all expenditures incurred by the agency in its operations and all repayments of loans made to the agency and payments of interest thereon.

(2) An agency may from time to time, out of any surplus funds standing to its credit in an account established pursuant to subsection (1), purchase, acquire and hold

(*a*) in the case of a federal agency, any securities of or guaranteed by the Government of Canada; and

(*b*) in the case of any other agency, any securities of or guaranteed by the Government of Canada, or of or guaranteed by the government of any province that is a party to the agreement pursuant to which the agency was authorized to be incorporated or was named.

(3) An agency may sell any securities purchased, acquired and held pursuant to subsection (2) and the proceeds of sale shall be deposited to the credit of the agency in the account established in respect of the agency under subsection (1).

Regulations

16.

(1) The Governor in Council may make regulations

(*a*) prescribing

(i) substances and classes of substances,

(ii) quantities or concentrations of substances and classes of substances in water, and

(iii) treatments, processes and changes of water

for the purpose of subsection 2 (2);

(*b*) prescribing the procedure to be followed by each agency in determining its recommendations as to charges that may be levied by it for treatment of waste at any waste treatment facility that is operated and maintained by the agency;

(c) prescribing the procedure to be followed by each agency in determining its recommendations as to water quality standards for waters comprising the water quality management area for which it is incorporated or named;

(d) prescribing the criteria, which shall be related to estimates of the cost of appropriate treatment of waste expected to be deposited, to be used by each agency in determining its recommendations as to effluent discharge fees to be paid by persons for the deposit of waste in waters comprising the water quality management area for which it is incorporated or named and the time or times at which and the manner in which such fees should be paid;

(e) requiring persons who deposit waste in any waters comprising a water quality management area to maintain books and records necessary for the proper enforcement of this Act and the regulations;

(f) requiring persons who have deposited waste in contravention of section 8 to report such deposit to the agency incorporated or named for the water quality management area in which the deposit is made and providing for the manner in which and the time within which such report is to be made;

(g) requiring persons who deposit waste in any waters comprising a water quality management area to submit test portions of such waste to the agency incorporated or named in respect of the area;

(h) respecting the method of analysis by each agency of test portions of waste submitted to it;

(i) respecting the powers and duties of inspectors and analysts, the taking of samples and the making of analyses for the purposes of this Act; and

(j) generally, for carrying out the purposes and provisions of this Act.

(2) Subject to subsection (3), the Governor in Council may make regulations prescribing, with respect to each water quality management area,

(a) the quantities, if any, of waste of any type that for the purposes of section 8, may be deposited in the waters comprising such area and the conditions under which any such waste may be deposited;

(*b*) the charges to be paid by any person to the agency incorporated or named in respect thereof

(i) for treatment of waste by the agency at a waste treatment facility that is operated and maintained by it, and
(ii) for analysis of waste samples by the agency,

and the persons by whom such charges are payable and the time or times at which and the manner in which such charges shall be paid;
(*c*) water quality standards for the waters comprising such area; and
(*d*) the effluent discharge fees, if any, to be paid by any person to the agency incorporated or named in respect thereof for the deposit of waste in the waters comprising such area and the persons by whom such fees are payable and the time or times at which and the manner in which such fees shall be paid.

(3) No regulation that is made by the Governor in Council under subsection (2) with respect to a water quality management area for which an agency is incorporated or named under an agreement entered into pursuant to section 9 is of any force or effect unless
(*a*) it is made on the recommendation of the agency, or
(*b*) where the Minister and the appropriate minister of each provincial government that is a party to the agreement disagree with the recommendations of the agency and jointly make a different recommendation, it is made on such joint recommendation.

PART III
Nutrients
Interpretation
17. In this Part and Part IV,
"cleaning agent" means any laundry detergent, dishwashing compound, household cleaner, metal cleaner, degreasing compound, commercial cleaner, industrial cleaner, phosphate compound or other substance intended to be used for cleaning purposes;
"nutrient" means any substance or combination of substances that, if added to any waters in sufficient quantities, provides nourishment that promotes the growth of aquatic vegetation in those waters to such densities as to

(*a*) interfere with their use by man or by any animal, fish or plant that is useful to man, or

(*b*) degrade or alter or form part of a process of degradation or alteration of the quality of those waters to an extent that is detrimental to their use by man or by any animal, fish or plant that is useful to man;

"water conditioner" means any water softening chemical, anti-scale chemical, corrosion inhibiter or other substance intended to be used to treat water.

Use of nutrients

18. No person shall manufacture for use or sale in Canada or import into Canada any cleaning agent or water conditioner that contains a prescribed nutrient in a concentration that is greater than the prescribed maximum permissible concentration of that nutrient in that cleaning agent or water conditioner.

Regulations

19. The Governor in Council may make regulations

(*a*) prescribing, for the purpose of section 18,

(i) nutrients, and

(ii) the maximum permissible concentration, if any, of any prescribed nutrient in any cleaning agent or water conditioner;

(*b*) respecting the manner in which the concentration of any prescribed nutrient in a cleaning agent or water conditioner shall be determined; and

(*c*) requiring persons who manufacture in Canada or import into Canada any cleaning agent or water conditioner

(i) to maintain books and records necessary for the proper enforcement of this Part and regulations made under this section, and

(ii) to submit samples of such cleaning agent or water conditioner to the Minister.

Seizure

20. (1) An inspector may at any reasonable time seize any cleaning agent or water conditioner that he reasonably believes has been manufactured in Canada or imported into Canada in violation of section 18.

(2) Any cleaning agent or water conditioner seized under this Act by an inspector may at the option of an inspector be kept or stored in the building or place where it was seized or may be removed to any other proper place by or at the direction of an inspector.

(3) Except with the authority of an inspector, no person shall remove, alter or interfere in any way with any cleaning agent or water conditioner seized under this Act by an inspector; but an inspector shall, at the request of a person from whom any cleaning agent or water conditioner was so seized, furnish a sample thereof to that person for analysis.

21. (1) Where any cleaning agent or water conditioner has been seized under this Act, any person may, within two months after the date of such seizure, upon prior notice having been given in accordance with subsection (2) to the Minister by registered mail addressed to him at Ottawa, apply to a magistrate within whose territorial jurisdiction the seizure was made for an order of restoration under subsection (3)

(2) The notice referred to in subsection (1) shall be mailed at least fifteen clear days prior to the day on which the application is to be made to the magistrate and shall specify
(*a*) the magistrate to whom the application is to be made;
(*b*) the place where and the time when the application is to be heard;
(*b*) the cleaning agent or water conditioner in respect of which the application is to be made; and
(*d*) the evidence upon which the applicant intends to rely to establish that he is entitled to possession of the cleaning agent or water conditioner in respect of which the application is to be made.

(3) Subject to section 22, where, upon the hearing of an application made under subsection (1), the magistrate is satisfied
(*a*) that the applicant is otherwise entitled to possession of the cleaning agent or water conditioner seized, and
(*b*) that the cleaning agent or water conditioner seized is not and

will not be required as evidence in any proceedings in respect of an offence under this Act,

he shall order that the cleaning agent or water conditioner seized be restored forthwith to the applicant, and where the magistrate is satisfied that the applicant is otherwise entitled to possession of the cleaning agent or water conditioner seized is not satisfied as to the matters mentioned in paragraph (*b*), he shall order that the cleaning agent or water conditioner seized be restored to the applicant

(*c*) upon the expiration of four months from the date of such seizure if no proceedings in respect of a violation of section 18 have been commenced before that time, or

(*d*) upon the final conclusion of any such proceedings in any other case.

(4) Where no application has been made under subsection (1) for the restoration of any cleaning agent or water conditioner seized under this Act within two months from the date of such seizure, or an application therefor has been made but upon the hearing thereof no order of restoration is made, the cleaning agent or water conditioner so seized shall be delivered to the Minister who may make such disposition thereof as he thinks fit.

22. (1) Where a person is convicted of an offence under subsection 28(1), any cleaning agent or water conditioner seized under this Act by mans of or in respect of which the offence was committed is thereupon forfeited to Her Majesty and shall be disposed of as the Minister directs.

(2) Where an inspector has seized any cleaning agent or water conditioner under this Act and the owner thereof or the person in whose possession it was at the time of seizure consents in writing to the destruction thereof, the cleaning agent or water conditioner is thereupon forfeited to Her Majesty's and shall be disposed of as the Minister directs.

PART IV
General
Inspectors and analysts

23. The Minister may designate any qualified person as an inspector or analyst for the purposes of this Act but where a qualified officer of any other department or agency of the Government of Canada carries out similar duties for the purposes of another Act the Minister shall designate such offer whenever possible.

24. (1) An inspector may at any reasonable time

(*a*) enter any area, place, premises, vessel or vehicle, other than a private dwelling place or any part of any such area, place, premises, vessel or vehicle that is designed to be used and is being used as a permanent or temporary private dwelling place, in which he reasonably believes

  (i) there is being or has been carried out any manufacturing or other process that may result in or has resulted in waste, or
  (ii) there is waste

that may be or has been added to any waters that have been designated as a water quality management area pursuant to section 9 or 11.

(*b*) enter any area, place, premises, vessel or vehicle, other than a private dwelling place or any part of any such area, place, premises, vessel or vehicle that is designed to be used and is being used as a permanent or temporary private dwelling place, in which he reasonably believes

  (i) any cleaning agent or water conditioner is being manufactured, or
  (ii) there is any cleaning agent or water conditioner that has been manufactured in Canada or imported into Canada in violation of section 18;

(*c*) examine any waste, cleaning agent or water conditioner found therein in bulk or open any container found therein that he has reason to believe contains any waste, cleaning agent or water conditioner and take samples thereof; and

(*d*) require any person in such area, place, premises, vehicle or vessel to produce for inspection or for the purpose of obtaining copies thereof or extracts therefrom, any books or other documents or papers concerning any matter relevant to the administration of this Act or the regulations.

(2) An inspector shall be furnished with a certificate of his designation as an inspector and on entering any area, place, premises, vehicle or vessel referred to in subsection (1) shall, if so required, produce the certificate to the person in charge thereof.

(3) The owner or person in charge of any area, place, premises, vehicle or vessel referred to in subsection (1) and every person found therein shall give an inspector all reasonable assistance in his power to enable the inspector to carry out his duties and functions under this Act and the regulations and shall furnish him with such information with respect to the administration of this Act and the regulations as he may reasonably require.

25. (1) No person shall obstruct or hinder an inspector in the carrying out of his duties or functions under this Act or the regulations.

(2) No person shall knowingly make a false or misleading statement, either verbally or in writing, to an inspector or other person engaged in carrying out his duties or functions under this Act or the regulations.

Advisory committees

26. (1) The Minister may establish and appoint the members of such advisory committees as he considers desirable for the purpose of advising and assisting him in carrying out the purposes and provisions of this Act.

(2) Each member of an advisory committee is entitled to be paid reasonable travelling and other expenses while absent from his ordinary place of residence in the course of his duties as such a member and may, with the approval of the Minister, be paid such amount as is fixed by the Governor in Council for each day he attends any meeting of the committee or for each day during which he performs, with the approval of the committee, any duties on behalf of the committee in addition to his ordinary duties as a member thereof.

Public information program

27. The Minister may, either directly or in cooperation with any government, institution or person, publish or otherwise distribute or arrange for the publication or distribution of such information as he deems necessary to inform the public respecting any aspect of the conservation, development or utilization of the water resources of Canada.

Offences

28. (1) Any person who violates section 8 or 18 is liable on summary conviction to a fine not exceeding five thousand dollars for each offence.

    (2) Where an offence under subsection (1) is committed on more than one day or is continued for more than one day, it shall be deemed to be a separate offence for each day on which the offence is committed or continued.

29. Any person who violates subsection 20(3) or section 25 or any regulation made under paragraph 16(1)(*e*), (*f*) or (*g*) or paragraph 19(*c*) is guilty of an offence punishable on summary conviction.

30. Where a person is convicted of an offence under this Act, the court may, in addition to any punishment it may impose, order that person to refrain from any further violation of the provision of the Act or regulations for the violation of which he has been convicted or to cease to carry on any activity specified in the order the carrying on of which, in the opinion of the court, will or is likely to result in any further violation thereof.

31. In a prosecution for an offence under this Act, it is sufficient proof of the offence to establish that it was committed by an employee or agent of the accused whether or not the employee or agent is identified or has been prosecuted for the offence, unless the accused establishes that the offence was committed without his knowledge or consent and that he exercised all due diligence to prevent its commission.

32. Proceedings in respect of an offence under this Act may be instituted at any time within two years after the time when the subject-matter of the proceedings arose.

33. Any complaint or information in respect of an offence under this Act may be heard, tried or determined by a court if the accused is resident or carrying on business within the territorial jurisdiction of that court although the matter of the complaint or information did not arise in that territorial jurisdiction.

34. (1) Notwithstanding that a prosecution has been instituted in respect of an offence under subsection 28(1) the Attorney General of Canada may commence and maintain proceedings to enjoin any violation of section 8.

(2) No civil remedy for any act or omission is suspended or affected by reason that the act or omission is an offence under this Act.

Evidence

35. (1) Subject to this section, a certificate of an analyst stating that he has analyzed or examined a sample submitted to him by an inspector and stating the result of his analysis or examination is admissible in evidence in any prosecution for a violation of this Act and in the absence of evidence to the contrary is proof of the statements contained in the certificate without proof of the signature or the official character of the person appearing to have signed the certificate.

(2) The party against whom a certificate of an analyst is produced pursuant to subsection (1) may, with leave of the court, require the attendance of the analyst for the purposes of cross-examination.

(3) No certificate shall be received in evidence pursuant to subsection (1) unless the party intending to produce it has given the party against whom it is intended to be produced reasonable notice of such intention together with a copy of the certificate.

Report to Parliament

36. The Minister shall, as soon as possible after the end of each fiscal year, prepare a report on the operations under this Act for that

year, and the Minister shall cause such report to be laid before Parliament forthwith upon the completion thereof, or, if Parliament is not then sitting, on any of the first fifteen days next thereafter that Parliament is sitting.

Financial

37. All expenditures by the Minister for the purposes of this Act shall be paid out of moneys appropriated by Parliament therefor.

38. Subject to section 37, the Minister may, with the approval of the Governor in Council,

(*a*) make loans or pay contributions to any agency in respect of the cost of incorporating the agency or in respect of its operating expenses or make loans to any agency in respect of capital costs incurred by it; and

(*b*) in accordance with an agreement entered into section 4, make loans or pay grants to the government of any province to meet any part of the portion of the cost of programs undertaken pursuant to such an agreement that is to be paid by the Minister.

APPLICATION

39. Section 8 is not applicable in respect of a water quality management area designated pursuant to section 9 or 11 until a proclamation has been issued declaring it to be applicable in respect of that area.

2. The Air Pollution Control Act, 1967

The Air Pollution Control Act, 1967

HER MAJESTY, by and with the advice and consent of the Legislative Assembly of the Province of Ontario, enacts as follows:

1. In this Act,

(*a*) "air contaminant" means a solid, liquid, gas, odour or combination of any of them that contributes to air pollution;

(*b*) "air pollution" means the presence in the outdoor atmosphere of any air contaminant or contaminants in quantities that may cause discomfort to or endanger the health or safety of persons, or that may cause injury or damage to property or to plant or animal life or that may interfere with visibility or the normal conduct of transport or business;

(*c*) "Board" means The Air Pollution Control Advisory Board;

(*d*) "construct" includes the erection, reconstruction, installation, alteration or modification of a stationary source of air pollution and the replacement of any part thereof, but does not include routine maintenance;

(*e*) "Department" means the Department of Energy and Resources Management;

(*f*) "Minister" means the Minister of Energy and Resources Management.

(*g*) "motor vehicle" means any self-propelled vehicle designed for transporting persons or property on a highway;

(*h*) "operator" means the person in occupation or having the charge, management or control of any land or premises on or in which a source of air pollution is located, whether on his own account or as the agent of any other person;

(*i*) "owner" includes the person for the time being receiving the rent of the land or premises on or in which a source of air pollution is located, whether on his own account or as agent or trustee of any other person;

(*j*) "provincial officer" means a person who is designated by the Minister as a provincial officer for the purposes of this Act and the regulations;

(*k*) "regulations" means the regulations made under this Act;

(*l*) "stationary source of air pollution" means any equipment, apparatus, device, mechanism or structure, except a motor vehicle, that may be a source of air pollution. R.S.O. 1960, c. 12, s.1(1), *amended.*

2. The Minister, for the purposes of the administration and enforcement of this Act and the regulations, may,

    (*a*) investigate air pollution problems;

    (*b*) conduct research in the field of air pollution;

    (*c*) conduct air quality and meteorological studies and monitoring programmes;

    (*d*) convene conferences, conduct seminars and educational programmes in the field of air pollution;

    (*e*) publish and disseminate information on air pollution;

    (*f*) make grants,

    (i) to universities and other organizations for research and training of persons in the field of air pollution, and

    (ii) to municipalities to assist in the administration and enforcement of air pollution by-laws,

    in such amounts and upon such terms and conditions as the regulations may prescribe;

    (*g*) appoint committees to perform such advisory functions as the Minister deems desirable. R.S.O. 1960, c. 12, s. 2, *amended.*

3. The Minister may authorize any officer or officers of the Department to exercise and discharge in his place any of the powers conferred or duties imposed upon him under this Act, except sections 6 and 10, or under the regulations. *New.*

4. (1) A board to be known as "The Air Pollution Control Advisory Board" shall be established consisting of not more than twelve members appointed by the Lieutenant Governor in Council as the regulations prescribe, one of whom may be designated as chairman and one as secretary.

    (2) The composition of the Board shall be such as to provide for competent and knowledgeable persons in the engineering, medical, urban planning, industry, agricultural and labour fields and members at large.

    (3) No member, servant or employee of the Board may serve until

he takes and subscribes before the Minister an oath of office and secrecy in the following form:

I,   ,
do swear that I will faithfully discharge my duties as a member of The Air Pollution Control Advisory Board and, except as I may be legally authorized or required, I will not disclose or give to any person any information or document that comes to my knowledge or possession by reason of my duties as a member of The Air Pollution Control Advisory Board.

So help me God.

(4) Vacancies in the membership of the Board may be filled by the Lieutenant Governor in Council.

(5) The Board shall review and report upon the recommendations of a provincial officer and perform such other duties and functions as the Minister may direct. 1961-62, c. 3, s. 1, *amended.*

5. (1) The Minister may designate officers of the Department as provincial officers for the purposes of this Act and the regulations.

(2) A provincial officer may enter in or upon any land or premises at any reasonable time and make or require to be made such examinations, tests and inquiries as may be necessary or advisable for the purposes of this Act or the regulations.

(3) Every operator and owner shall furnish such information as a provincial officer requires for the purposes of this Act or the regulations. R.S.O. 1960, c. 12, s. 7, *amended.*

(4) No person shall obstruct a provincial officer in the exercise of his powers under this section.

6. (1) Any person who complains that it is not feasible or practicable to comply with a certificate of approval or order issued or made under this Act may request the Minister to review the certificate or order, and the Minister may review, rescind or alter any such certificate or order. R.S.O. 1960, c. 12, s. 8, *amended.*

(2) If after a review by the Minister any person complains that it is still not feasible or practicable to comply with the certificate of approval or order, he may, within fifteen days after receipt of the decision of the Minister, appeal to a judge of the county or district

court of the county or district in which the source of air pollution in respect of which the certificate or order was issued or made is located, and such appeal shall be a hearing *de novo,* and the judge may dismiss the appeal or rescind or alter any such certificate or order and his decision is final. *New.*

7. (1) No person shall construct a stationary source of air pollution unless he has obtained from the Minister a certificate of approval to the method and devices to be employed to control the emission of any air contaminant into the outdoor atmosphere from the source and to prevent air pollution.

(2) An applicant for a certificate of approval shall submit to the Minister such plans, specifications and other information with respect to the source of air pollution as the Minister may require.

(3) The Minister may issue a certificate of approval subject to such terms and conditions respecting the method and devices to be employed for the control of the emission of any air contaminant into the outdoor atmosphere from the source of air pollution, and for the prevention of air pollution as the Minister deems necessary. *New.*

(4) No person shall construct a stationary source of air pollution except in accordance with the plans, specifications, methods and devices in respect of which the certificate of approval was issued.

(5) A certificate of approval expires one year after it is issued unless the construction in respect of which it was issued has commenced before that time.

8. (8) A provincial officer may survey from time to time any source of air pollution and after completing such survey shall report thereon with his recommendations,

(*a*) respecting the stationary source of air pollution and such method of operation and devices as may be necessary to prevent or lessen the emission of any air contaminant into the outdoor atmosphere;

(*b*) respecting the source of air pollution where no equipment, apparatus, device, mechanism or structure is involved and such method of operation as may be necessary to prevent or lessen the emission of any air contaminant into the outdoor atmosphere; or (c) respecting the air pollution caused by the concentration of motor vehicles at passenger, repair or storage depots or other places where motor vehicles are marshalled, housed or parked and such methods of operation and devices as may be necessary to prevent or lessen the emission of air contaminants.

(2) The provincial officer shall file his report and recommendations with the Department and shall serve upon the operator or owner of the source of air pollution a copy thereof.

(3) Upon receipt of a request in writing of the operator or owner filed with the secretary of the Board not later than fourteen days after the operator or owner received a copy of the report and recommendations, the Board shall review the report and recommendations of the provincial officer and, before it reports thereon with its recommendations, the Board shall provide the Minister and the operator or owner with an opportunity of appearing before it at a hearing to be held not earlier than fourteen days after notice has been served on the Minister and the operator or owner stating the time and place of the hearing.

(4) Upon a hearing, the parties are entitled to be present and to be represented by counsel and make such representations as they desire.

(5) The Board shall send its report and recommendations to the Minister and shall forthwith serve a copy thereof upon the operator or owner. *New.*

9. (1) Upon receipt of the report and recommendations of a provincial officer or, if such a report and recommendations are reviewed by the Board, upon receipt of the report and recommendations of the Board, the Minister may make such order as he deems necessary for prohibiting the operation of the source of air pollution or requiring changes respecting the source of air pollution or the method of operation or devices employed to prevent or lessen the emission of any air contaminant or to reduce or control air pollution.

(2) No order in respect of a source of air pollution shall be made under subsection 1 until fourteen days have elapsed after the report and recommendations of a provincial officer have been received by the operator or owner of the source of air pollution. *New.*

10. (1) Whenever the Minister, after investigation, is of the opinion that any person is emitting or causing to be emitted into the out-door atmosphere any air contaminant that constitutes a serious danger to the health of any persons and that it would be prejudicial to the interests of such persons to delay action to complete a sur-vey under section 8, he shall notify the person by a written order that he must immediately discontinue the emission of such con-taminant into the outdoor atmosphere, including reasons thereof, whereupon such person shall immediately discontinue such emission.

(2) The Minister shall, as soon as possible thereafter and in any event not later than seven days after giving such notice, provide the person with an opportunity to be heard and to present any evi-dence that such emission does not constitute a serious danger to the health of any persons. *New.*

11. (1) Where a person complains that air pollution is causing or has caused injury or damage to live stock or to crops, trees or other vegetation which may result in economic loss to such person, he may, within fourteen days after the injury or damage becomes apparent, request the minister to conduct an investigation.

(2) Upon receipt of a request, the Minister may cause an investiga-tion to be made and a report prepared of the findings of the in-vestigation.

(3) A copy of the report shall be given to the claimant and to the operator or owner of the source of air pollution alleged to be the cause of the injury or damage.

(4) The claimant shall permit the operator or owner of such source of air pollution or his agent to view the injury or damage and to remove samples and conduct tests and examinations as may

be reasonably necessary to establish the cause of the injury or damage.

(5) A board of negotiation shall be established consisting of two or more members appointed by the Lieutenant Governor in Council, one of whom may be designated as chairman.

(6) Any two members of the board of negotiation constitute a quorum and are sufficient to perform all the functions of the board on behalf of the board.

(7) The board of negotiation may sit at any place in Ontario.

(8) If a complainant who has requested an investigation under subsection 1 desires to have his claim for injury or damage negotiated by the board of negotiation, he shall notify the Minister and the operator or owner of the source of air pollution alleged to be the cause of the injury or damage of the amount of his claim within a reasonable time after the amount can be determined.

(9) If the claimant and the operator or owner are not able to settle the claim within thirty days after notice of the claim is given to the Minister under subsection 8, the claimant or the operator or owner may serve notice of negotiation upon the other of them and upon the board of negotiation stating that he requires a settlement of the claim to be negotiated by the board of negotiation.

(10) Upon receipt of a notice of negotiation, the board of negotiation shall assess the injury or damage in respect of which the claim is made and, upon reasonable notice to the claimant and to the operator or owner, shall meet with them and, without prejudice to any subsequent proceedings, proceed in a summary and informal manner to negotiate a settlement of the claim.

(ii) This section does not apply to injury or damage caused by sulphur fumes arising from the operations designated in *The Damage by Fumes Arbitration Act. New.*

12. (1) No person shall sell, offer or expose for sale a new motor vehicle or new motor vehicle engine of a class or type that is required by the regulations to have installed on or incorporated in it

any system or device to prevent or lessen the emission into the outdoor atmosphere of any air contaminant or contaminants unless such motor vehicle complies with the regulations.

(2) Every person who contravenes any provision of this section is guilty of an offence and on summary conviction is liable to a fine of not less than $50 and not more than $500. *New.*

13. (1) No person shall operate a motor vehicle of a class or type that is required by the regulations to have installed on or incorporated in it any system or device to prevent or lessen the emission into the outdoor atmosphere of any air contaminant or contaminants unless such motor vehicle has installed on or incorporated in it such system or device and makes effective use of such system or device.

(2) Every person who contravenes any provision of this section is guilty of an offence and on summary conviction is liable to a fine of not more than $100. *New.*

14. (1) The Lieutenant Governor in Council may make regulations,
(*a*) classifying sources of air pollution and exempting any class or classes from the provisions of this Act and the regulations;
(*b*) classifying motor vehicles and motor vehicle engines for the purpose of any regulation and exempting any class or type of motor vehicle or motor vehicle engine from any regulation;
(*c*) requiring motor vehicles or any class or type thereof and motor vehicle engines or any class or type thereof to have installed thereon or incorporated therein one or more systems or devices to prevent or lessen the emission into the outdoor atmosphere of any air contaminant or contaminants, prescribing the standards and specifications of any such system or device, prescribing the standards of emission into the outdoor atmosphere of any air contaminant or contaminants to which any such system or device shall comply and providing for the testing and inspection of any such system or device;
(*ca*) providing for the issuance by the Minister of certificates of approval of systems or devices proposed to be installed on or incorporated in motor vehicles to prevent or lessen emission into the outdoor atmosphere of air contaminant or contaminants.

(*d*) defining and designating new motor vehicles and new motor vehicle engines for the purpose of any regulation;

(*e*) prohibiting or regulating and controlling the emission of any air contaminant or contaminants into the outdoor atmosphere from any source of air pollution or any class thereof;

(*f*) regulating the quality of fuels that may be used for heating, generating steam or electricity or for industrial processes;

(*g*) designating the areas in Ontario to which this Act and the regulations are applicable and designating the date on which this Act and the regulations become effective in any area;

(*h*) prescribing the composition, quorum and practice and procedure of the Board and the terms of office and remuneration of its members;

(*i*) prescribing the amounts of grants payable to universities and municipalities, and the terms and conditions of such grants;

(*j*) prescribing the ambient air quality criteria to be used in controlling, regulating or prohibiting the emission of any air contaminant or contaminants into the outdoor atmosphere and the standards thereof;

(*k*) respecting any matter necessary or advisable to carry out effectively the intent and purpose of this Act.

(2) Any regulation may be general or particular in its application and may be limited as to time or place or both. R.S.O. 1960, c. 12, s. 6, *amended.*

15. Notwithstanding any general or special Act, this Act and the regulations apply in such areas in Ontario as are designated by the regulations. *New.*

16. (1) Every person who contravenes any provision of this Act, except section 12 or 13, or of the regulations or any order of the Minister made under this Act or the regulations, is guilty of an offence and on summary conviction is liable, if an individual, to a fine of not more than $2,000, and, if a corporation, on first conviction to a fine of not more than $5,000 and on each subsequent conviction to a fine of not more than $10,000.

(2) Each day that a person contravenes a provision of this Act or

the regulations or an order made by the Minister constitutes a separate offence. R.S.O. 1960, c. 12, s. 9; 1966, c. 5, s. 1, *amended.*

17. Any report, order or notice served under this Act shall be deemed to be sufficiently served if it or a copy thereof is delivered to the operator of the source of air pollution in respect of which the report, order or notice is served, or is delivered,
(*a*) in the case of a municipality, including a metropolitan municipality, to the head or clerk of the municipality;
(*b*) in the case of any other corporation, to the president, vice-president, manager, treasurer, secretary, clerk or agent of the corporation or of any branch or agency thereof in Ontario;
(*c*) in the case of a firm or partnership, to any member thereof, or, at the last known place of abode of any such member, to any adult member of his household, or, at the office or place of business of the firm or partnership, to a clerk employed therein; or
(*d*) in the case of an individual, to him, or, at his last known place of abode, to any adult member of his household, or, at his office or place of business, to a clerk employed therein. *New.*

18. Every air pollution control by-law of a municipality, including a metropolitan municipality, passed under *The Air Pollution Control Act* or *The Municipal Act,* that is in force immediately before this Act and the regulations become effective in the municipality, and *The Air Pollution Control Act* and the amendments thereto referred to in section 19 shall remain in force in the municipality until this Act and the regulations become effective in the municipality. *New.*

19. Subject to section 18, the following are repealed:
1 *The Air Pollution Control Act.*
2 *The Air Pollution Control Amendment Act, 1961-62.*
3 *The Air Pollution Control Amendment Act, 1962-63.*
4 *The Air Pollution Control Amendment Act, 1966.*

20. This Act comes into force on a day to be named by the Lieutenant Governor by his proclamation.

21. This Act may be cited as *The Air Pollution Control Act, 1967.*

Ontario Regulation 18/70: Evaporative emissions from new light duty motor vehicles

1. In this Regulation,

   (*a*) "engine displacement" means the product, expressed in cubic inches, resulting from the multiplication of the total cross-sectional area of the cylinders of the motor vehicle engine, as expressed in square inches, and the piston stroke, as expressed in inches;

   (*b*) "evaporative emissions" means any hydro-carbon component of motor gasoline emitted to the outdoor atmosphere from the fuel tank or carburetor of a light duty motor vehicle;

   (*c*) "exhaust emissions" means air contaminant or contaminants emitted to the outdoor atmosphere from any opening downstream from the exhaust port of a light duty motor vehicle engine;

   (*d*) "gross vehicle weight" means the manufacturer's gross weight rating;

   (*e*) "light commercial motor vehicle" means a commercial motor vehicle as defined in *The Highway Traffic Act*.

       (i) that has a gross vehicle weight of not more than 6,000 pounds.

       (ii) that is manufactured after the commencement of the 1971 model year of the manufacturer, and

       (iii) for which a motor vehicle permit is issued by the Ontario Department of Transport;

   (*f*) "light duty motor vehicle" means a passenger motor vehicle or a light commercial motor vehicle;

   (*g*) "model" in respect of a new light duty motor vehicle means a class of motor vehicle designed, constructed and assembled by the manufacturer thereof for a particular purpose and designated as a model by the manufacturer during a model year;

   (*h*) "model year" means the annual period of manufacturing of new light duty motor vehicles or new light duty motor vehicle engines, in the twelve month period designated by the manufacturer, but, where the manufacturer does not so designate such motor vehicle and motor vehicle engines, the model year in respect of such motor vehicles and motor vehicle engines means the twelve-month period beginning on the 1st day of January of the year in which such manufacturing begins;

(*i*) "motorcycle" means a self-propelled motor vehicle having a seat or saddle for the use of the driver and designed to travel on not more than three wheels in contact with the ground and includes a bicycle with a motor attached and a motor scooter, but does not include any motor vehicle that weighs at least 1,500 pounds;

(*j*) "passenger motor vehicle" means a motor vehicle other than a motorcycle or a bus,

(i) that is designed to carry an operator and one or more passengers,

(ii) that is manufactured after the commencement of the 1971 model year of the manufacturer, and

(iii) for which a motor vehicle permit is issued by the Ontario Department of Transport;

(*k*) "system or device" includes any modification of a motor vehicle having a motor vehicle engine, which modification prevents or lessens the emission of air contaminant or contaminants into the outdoor atmosphere;

(*l*) "ultimate purchaser" means the person to whom a motor vehicle permit for the operation of a motor vehicle or motor vehicle engine is issued by the Ontario Department of Transport.

APPLICATION

2. This Regulation applies to new light duty motor vehicles manufactured after the commencement of the 1971 model year and sold, offered or exposed for sale to or used by the ultimate purchaser who is a resident of Ontario.

EXEMPTIONS

3. The classes and types of new motor vehicles exempt from this Regulation are,

(*a*) a motor vehicle having a motor vehicle engine that has an engine displacement of less than fifty cubic inches;

(*b*) a motor vehicle that has a gross vehicle weight of more than 6,000 pounds;

(*c*) a motorcycle;

(*d*) a motor vehicle or motor vehicle engine not intended for use on a street or highway;

(e) a motor vehicle that is operated by a person not a resident of Ontario who is in Ontario temporarily;

(f) a new light duty motor vehicle that uses fuel other than gasoline or compressed or liquefied hydrocarbons for motive power;

(g) new light duty motor vehicles having new light duty motor vehicle engines of a specified engine displacement of which not more than fifty such new light duty motor vehicles having new light duty motor vehicle engines are sold or delivered in Ontario in any model year; or

(h) any new light duty motor vehicle, having a new light duty motor vehicle engine, forming part of a manufacturer's total annual sales volume in Ontario, where such total annual sales volume does not exceed 100 new light duty motor vehicle engines.

EVAPORATIVE EMISSIONS

4. (1) For the purposes of this section,

(a) where the records of a manufacturer of his sales in Ontario of new light duty motor vehicles in any year are not available or are inadequate for the selection of new light duty motor vehicles and new light duty motor vehicle engines for a model year for testing under subsection 5, the manufacturer shall make selections of new light duty motor vehicles and new light duty motor vehicle engines on the basis of his total sales of new light duty motor vehicles and new light duty motor vehicle engines; or

(b) where any motor vehicle manufacturer is subject to the terms and conditions of the Canada-U.S. Automotive Products Trade Agreement, he may, when selecting new light duty motor vehicles and new light duty motor vehicle engines for a model year for testing under subsection 5, base his selection on the records of his sales for the area covered by the Agreement.

(2) Where a new light duty motor vehicle is tested prior to the application by a manufacturer for approval to sell new light duty motor vehicles in Ontario, the evaporative emissions from such motor vehicle shall not exceed 6 grams of hydrocarbons per test.

(3) The requirements of subsection 2 apply to a composite value calculated under subsection 7 from results obtained in tests of

evaporative emissions from the operation of the new light duty
motor vehicles in accordance with the test procedures set out in
paragraphs 3, 4 and 5 of subsection 5.

(4) Where the composite value calculated under subsection 7 for a
new light duty motor vehicle having a new light duty motor vehicle
engine of a specified engine displacement does not exceed the
amount of hydrocarbon evaporative emissions set out in subsection 2, every new light duty motor vehicle having a new light
duty motor vehicle engine of that specified engine displacement
shall be deemed to comply with the requirements of subsection 2.

(5) Procedures for selecting, testing and inspecting evaporative
emission control systems or devices installed on or incorporated in
new light duty motor vehicles to prevent or lessen the emission
into the outdoor atmosphere of evaporative emissions from the
operation of such new light duty motor vehicles, shall be as follows:

1 Where a manufacturer of new light duty motor vehicles and
new light duty motor vehicle engines intends to sell, offer or expose for sale in any model year a new light duty motor vehicle
having a new light duty motor vehicle engine, he shall select, from
his manufacture of such light duty motor vehicles and light duty
motor vehicle engines, for testing of evaporative emissions,
(a) at least two such new light duty motor vehicles having new
light duty motor vehicle engines of the same engine displacement;
and
(b) where the probable sales volume of new light duty motor
vehicles having new light duty motor vehicle engines of a specified
engine displacement will account for at least one-half of one per
cent of the total number of new light duty motor vehicles sold in
Ontario in the latest preceding model year of the manufacturer for
which sales records in Ontario are available, at least four new light
duty motor vehicles having new light duty motor vehicle engines of
the same engine displacement,
but in no case shall the total number of new light duty motor
vehicles having new light duty motor vehicle engines be fewer than
four.

2 The combinations of new light duty motor vehicles and new
light duty motor vehicle engines selected under paragraph 1 and

used for the testing of evaporative emissions shall be those combinations usually produced for sale by the manufacturer and shall be equipped as nearly as possible with transmission and carburetors in proportion to the number of comparable new light duty motor vehicles so equipped in the latest preceding model year of the manufacturer for which is sales records in Ontario are available.

3 Each new light duty motor vehicle having a new light duty motor vehicle engine selected for testing under paragraph 1 for amounts of evaporative emissions shall be driven a distance of at least 4,000 miles with all evaporative emission control systems or devices installed and operating and tests shall then be made for the amounts of evaporative emissions as described in paragraph 4.

4 Each test shall consist of three parts which shall be performed in sequence and without any interruption between each part, by,

(a) installing previously weighed hydrocarbon vapour collection devices on all fuel system external vents, then heating, by artificial means, the fuel in the tank of the new light duty motor vehicle to a temperature of between 82 and 86 degrees Farenheit over a period of not less than 50 minutes and not more than 70 minutes, after which time the new light duty motor vehicle shall be moved on to a dynamometer;

(b) running the new light duty motor vehicle on a dynamometer and the motor vehicle engine for each test being run from a cold start through nine identical testing cycles without stalling of the new light duty motor vehicle engine and with each cycle lasting 137 seconds and consisting of a series of periods of acceleration, deceleration, steady speeds and idling; and

(c) permitting the new light duty motor vehicle to stand for a period of one hour at an ambient temperature, between 76 and 86 degrees Fahrenheit, after which time the hydrocarbon vapour collection devices shall be removed from the vehicle and sealed.

5 The evaporative emission referred to in paragraph 3 shall be obtained by re-weighing the previously weighed hydrocarbon vapour collection devices and the increase of weight of such devices shall be recorded in respect of each new light duty motor vehicle so that a value, expressed as grams of hydrocarbons per test, is obtained for that vehicle and engine for the purposes of subsection 7.

6 In addition to the selection of new light duty motor vehicles having new light duty motor vehicle engines for testing of evaporative emissions under paragraphs 2 to 5, the manufacturer shall select not fewer than four and not more than twelve new light duty motor vehicles for tests of durability of the evaporative emission control systems or devices and in the selection he shall have regard to the combinations of engine displacements and transmissions, including automatic and manual transmission installations, so that his selections represent at least 70 per cent of the number of new light duty motor vehicles sold by the manufacturer in Ontario during his latest preceding model year for which his sales records in Ontario are available, but where his records show that the total number of new light duty motor vehicles sold by him in Ontario is less than 10 per cent of the total sales in Ontario of all new light duty motor vehicles of all manufacturers, the combinations shall be so chosen that the number of new light duty motor vehicles tested for durability of the evaporative emission control systems or devices shall be not fewer than four and not more than eight and shall represent at least 50 per cent of the number of new light duty motor vehicles sold by the manufacturer during such model year.

7 Every new light duty motor vehicle having a new light duty motor vehicle engine selected under paragraph 6 shall be driven a distance of at least 50,000 miles and tested in the manner referred to in paragraph 4, the tests to be carried out on each new light duty motor vehicle at intervals of not more than 4,000 miles, and the results from such tests shall be recorded.

8 From the results recorded under paragraph 7, a value shall be calculated for the evaporative emissions during each test for each 4,000 mile interval for each new light duty motor vehicle in the manner described in paragraph 5 and the representative values thus obtained shall be used in the calculation of the factor mentioned in subsection 7.

(6) Where recording is made in this section of results of tests for amounts of evaporative emissions in respect of any new light duty motor vehicle having a new light duty motor vehicle engine, a composite value shall be determined under subsection 7 for each engine displacement, which composite value takes into account factors of deterioration in efficiency of the evaporative emission control

system or device installed thereon or incorporated therein, resulting from the use of that new light duty motor vehicle and new light duty motor vehicle engine, in accordance with the procedure under subsection 7.

(7) The procedure for the calculation of the composite value of the evaporative emissions of each new light duty motor vehicle tested shall be as follows:

1 For each combination of exhaust emission control system or device and evaporative emission control system or device, an evaporative emission deterioration factor shall be determined by using the results obtained from the relevant new light duty motor vehicles and new light duty motor vehicle engines tested under paragraphs 7 and 8 of subsection 5 by,

(a) plotting a graph for each combination of exhaust emission control system or device and evaporative emission control system or device of vehicle mileage against the evaporative emission values obtained in the tests under paragraphs 7 and 8 of subsection 5;

(b) drawing a straight line, by the method of least squares, as near as possible to the points plotted on each graph; and

(c) calculating the deterioration factor in respect of evaporative emissions for deterioration in efficiency for each combination of exhaust emission control system or device and evaporative emission control system or device in accordance with the following formula:

Factor = evaporative emissions interpolated to 50,000 miles minus evaporative emissions interpolated to 4,000 miles.

2 The evaporative emission test results from each new light duty motor vehicle tested under paragraphs 3, 4 and 5 of subsection 5 shall be added to the appropriate factor determined in paragraph 1 of this subsection for the particular engine displacement of that new light duty motor vehicle.

3 For each engine displacement, the results obtained in paragraph 2 for each new light duty motor vehicle in that engine displacement class shall be weighted in proportion to the projected sales of the new light duty motor vehicles represented by each test vehicle.

4 For each engine displacement, the weighted results obtained in paragraph 3 shall be averaged.

5 For each engine displacement, the evaporative emissions to be compared with the standard, referred to in subsection 2, shall be the averaged value for evaporative emissions obtained under paragraph 4 of this subsection.

Ontario Regulation 133/70: General

INTERPRETATION
1. In this Regulation,
   (*a*) "air pollution episode" means an occasion when air contamination is at such a level and for such a period of time that the air contamination may become the cause of increased human sickness and mortality;
   (*b*) "air pollution index" means a series of numbers expressing the relative levels of air pollution and taking into consideration one or more air contaminants;
   (*c*) "dust separation equipment" includes any device that separates solid material from the gaseous medium in which it is carried;
   (*d*) "equipment" includes apparatus, device, mechanism or structure;
   (*e*) "fuel burning equipment designed to burn fuel but does not include an internal combustion engine;
   (*f*) "incinerator" includes equipment used for the burning of waste;
   (*g*) "odour" includes the smell of ammonia, hydrogen sulphide, skatol, sulphur dioxide or other smell that causes discomfort to persons;
   (*h*) "smoke density" means the shade or opacity of smoke at or near the point of emission to the atmosphere;
   (*i*) "smoke density chart" means the chart described in section 7 for the purpose of determining smoke density under this Regulation.

APPLICATION
2. The Act and this Regulation apply to all areas within Ontario.

EXEMPTIONS
3. The following sources of air pollution are classified and are exempt from the provisions of section 7 of the Act requiring the obtaining of a certificate of approval from the Minister:
   Fuel burning equipment used solely for the purpose of comfort heating in,
      i. dwellings used for the housing of not more than three families, or

ii. commercial establishments having less than 35,000 cubic feet of space.

2 Construction equipment for construction and maintenance of public roads while the equipment is on the road.

3 Equipment for the preparation of food for on-site human consumption.

4 A bakery supplying not more than one retail outlet.

5 A dry cleaning establishment serving not more than one retail outlet.

6 Equipment for seeding, harvesting, fertilizing or for pest or weed control on agricultural lands.

AIR POLLUTION INDEX

4. (1) The Department may prepare an index to be known as the "Air Pollution Index" for any area in Ontario, from time to time.

(2) Where the air pollution index for an area indicates increasing air pollution that may lead to an air pollution episode, the Minister, in consultation with the Minister of Health, may order curtailment of the operation of sources of air pollution in the manner described in subsections 3 and 4.

(3) Where the air pollution index reaches the number 32, designated as Air Advisory Level, and meteorological forecasts indicate a six hour prolongation of atmospheric conditions conducive to sustained or increased air pollution levels, the Minister may require owners or operators of sources of air pollution to make preparation for the curtailment of such operations as are specified by the Minister.

(4) Where the air pollution index reaches the number 50, designated as First Air Pollution Alert, and meteorological forecasts indicate a six hour prolongation of atmospheric conditions conducive to sustained or increased air pollution levels, the Minister may require owners or operators of sources of air pollution to curtail such operations as are specified by the Minister.

CONTROL OF AIR CONTAMINANTS

5. (1) The standards for concentrations of air contaminants from stationary sources of air pollution at a point of impingement are

prescribed in Schedule 1.

(2) For the air contaminant mentioned in column 1, the amount thereof in the atmosphere at the point of impingement measured or calculated in accordance with column 2 shall not be greater than the amount shown in column 3 for the period of time shown in column 4 of Schedule 1.

(3) No person shall operate or cause to be operated any stationary source of air pollution in a manner that does not comply with the standards prescribed in Schedule 1.

6. No person shall cause or permit to be caused the emission of any air contaminant to such extent or degree as may,
   (a) cause discomfort to persons;
   (b) cause loss of enjoyment of normal use of property;
   (c) interfere with normal conduct of business; or
   (d) cause damage to property.

7. (1) The Department shall prepare a chart to be known as the "Smoke Density Chart of the Province of Ontario".

   (2) The smoke density chart shall be prepared by the recording, in five consecutive areas on the chart, of fine black dots or lines evenly spaced on a white background in such manner that,
   (a) approximately 20 per cent of the space in the first area is black, such area to be designated density No. 1;
   (b) approximately 40 per cent of the space in the second area is black, such area to be designated density No. 2;
   (c) approximately 60 per cent of the space in the third area is black, such area to be designated density No. 3;
   (d) approximately 80 per cent of the space in the fourth area is black, such area to be designated density No. 4; and
   (e) approximately 100 per cent of the space in the fifth area is black, such area to be designated density No. 5.

   (3) For the purpose of enforcing the Act and this Regulation, no person other than a provincial officer shall determine smoke density by a smoke density chart.

   (4) Where the density or opacity of smoke is determined, the

smoke is deemed to be of the density on the smoke density chart that it most closely resembles and to have the density number designated on the chart for such density.

8. (1) Subject to subsections 2 and 3, no person shall cause or permit to be caused the emission of smoke having a density or opacity greater than density No. 1.

(2) For a period of not more than four minutes in the aggregate in each half hour period, smoke may have a density or opacity not exceeding density No. 2.

(3) Where a new fire is started in any fuel-burning equipment, the smoke may have a density or opacity not exceeding density No. 3 for a period or periods of not more than three minutes in the aggregate in each quarter hour period.

9. Where at any stationary source of air pollution a failure to operate in the normal manner or a change in operating conditions occurs, or a shut-down of the source or part thereof is made for some purpose, resulting in the emission of air contaminants that may result in quantities or concentrations in excess of those allowed in sections 5, 6 and 8,
(*a*) the owner or operator of the source of air pollution shall,
(i) immediately notify a provincial officer and furnish him with particulars of such failure, change or shut-down, and
(ii) furnish the provincial officer with the particulars in writing, as soon as is practicable, of such failure, change or shut-down; and
(*b*) the provincial officer, where he deems it advisable, may authorize, in writing, the continuance of such operation for such period of time as he deems reasonable in the circumstances and may impose upon the owner or operator such terms and conditions for such continued operation as he deems necessary in the circumstances.

10. (1) No person shall burn or permit to be burned in any fuel burning equipment or incinerator any fuel or waste except the fuel or waste for the burning of which the equipment or incinerator was designed.

(2) No person shall burn or permit to be burned in any fuel burning equipment or incinerator any fuel or waste at a greater rate than that rate for which the equipment or incinerator was designed.

11. (1) Subject to subsection 2, no person shall burn or permit to be burned any material in an open fire that may contribute to air pollution except with the permission and under the direction of a provincial officer.

(2) A person may burn or permit to be burned material in an open fire where the fire is for recreational purposes, provided that the fire does not contribute to air pollution.

12. No person shall store, handle or transport any solid, liquid or gaseous material or substance in such manner than an air contaminant is released to the atmosphere.

13. Except with the permission and direction of a provincial officer, no person shall operate or cause to be operated an incinerator other than a municipally operated incinerator at any time other than between the hours of 7 a.m. and 5 p.m. during any day.

14. The Minister may require the installation of such devices or methods as are necessary to record the periods of operation of process, combustion or control equipment, which records shall be available to a provincial officer.

15. No person shall operate fuel burning equipment designed for the burning of solid fuel in suspension unless dust separating equipment is installed and operating in conjunction with the fuel burning equipment.

AIR QUALITY

16. For the purpose of attaining a high quality environment, the Minister shall use the values prescribed in Schedule 2 for controlling ambient air quality.

17. Ontario Regulation 449/67 and Ontario Regulations 45/68,

188/68, 281/68, 299/68, 437/68, 52/69, 186/69, 224/69 and 478/69 are revoked.

Schedule 1

Standards for emitted contaminants

Item	COLUMN 1 Name of contaminant	COLUMN 2 Units of concentration	COLUMN 3 Amount of concentration at point of impingement	COLUMN 4 Period of time
1	Ammonia	parts of ammonia per one million parts of air by volume	5.0 average	30 minutes
2	Beryllium	micrograms of beryllium per cubic metre of air	0.01 average	30 minutes
3	Bromine	parts of bromine per one million parts of air by volume	0.01 average	30 minutes
4	Cadmium Oxide	micrograms of cadmium oxide per cubic metre of air	10 average	30 minutes
5	Carbon Bisulphide	parts of carbon bisulphide per one million parts of air by volume	0.15 average	30 minutes
6	Carbon Monoxide	parts of carbon monoxide per one million parts of air by volume	5.0 average	30 minutes
7	Chlorine	parts of chlorine per one million parts of air by volume	0.1 average	30 minutes
8	Dustfall	tons of dustfall per square mile	15 total	30 days
9	Fluorides	parts of fluorides per one billion parts of air by volume	5.0 average	30 minutes
10	Hydrogen Chloride	parts of hydrogen chloride per one million parts of air by volume	0.04 average	30 minutes
11	Hydrogen Cyanide	parts of hydrogen cyanide per one million parts of air by volume	1.0 average	30 minutes
12	Hydrogen Sulphide	parts of hydrogen sulphide per one million parts of air by volume	0.03 average	30 minutes
13	Iron	micrograms of iron per cubic metre of air	10 average	30 minutes

Schedule 1— *Continued*

Standards for emitted contaminants

Item	COLUMN 1 Name of contaminant	COLUMN 2 Units of concentration	COLUMN 3 Amount of concentration at point of impingement	COLUMN 4 Period of time
14	Lead	micrograms of lead per cubic metre of air	20 average	30 minutes
15	Lime	micrograms of lime per cubic metre of air	20 average	30 minutes
16	Nitric Acid	micrograms of nitric acid per cubic metre of air	65 average	30 minutes
17	Nitrogen Oxides	parts of nitrogen oxides per one million parts of air by volume	0.25 average	30 minutes
18	Silver	micrograms of silver per cubic metre of air	1 average	30 minutes
19	Sulphur Dioxide	parts of sulphur dioxide per one million parts of air by volume	0.3 average	30 minutes
20	Suspended particulate	micrograms of suspended particulate matter per cubic metre of air	100 average	30 minutes

Schedule 2

Criteria for desirable ambient air quality

Item	COLUMN 1 Name of contaminant	COLUMN 2 Units of concentration	COLUMN 3 Amount of concentration in ambient air or forage	COLUMN 4 Period of time
1	Beryllium	micrograms of beryllium per cubic metre of air	0.01 average	24 hours
2	Carbon Monoxide	parts of carbon monoxide per one million parts of air by volume	40 average 15 average 8 average	1 hour 8 hours 24 hours
3	Dustfall	tons of dustfall per square mile	20 total 13 monthly average	30 days 1 year

Schedule 2— *Continued*

Criteria for desirable ambient air quality

Item	Name of contaminant	Units of concentration	Amount of concentration in ambient air or forage	Period of time
	COLUMN 1	COLUMN 2	COLUMN 3	COLUMN 4
4	Fluorides	parts of fluorides per one billion parts of air by volume	1.0 average 0.5 average	24 hours 30 days
5	Fluorides in forage for consumption by livestock	parts of fluorides per one million parts forage (dry weight)	35 total	individual sample
6	Fluoridation	micrograms of fluorides per 100 square centimetres	40 total	30 days
7	Hydrogen Sulphide	parts of hydrogen sulphide per one million parts of air by volume	0.02 average	1 hour
8	Lead	micrograms of lead per cubic metre of air	15 average 10 average	24 hours 30 days
9	Lime	micrograms of lime per cubic metre of air	10 average	24 hours
10	Oxidants	parts of oxidants per one million parts of air by volume	0.10 average 0.03 average	1 hour 24 hours
11	Oxides of Nitrogen	parts of oxides of nitrogen per one million parts of air by volume	0.20 average 0.10 average	1 hour 24 hours
12	Soiling	co-efficient of haze per 1000 feet of air	1.0 average 0.45 average	24 hours 1 year
13	Sulphation	milligrams of sulphur trioxide per 100 square centimetres	0.4 average per day	30 days
14	Sulphur Dioxide	parts of sulphur dioxide per one million parts of air by volume	0.25 average 0.10 average 0.02 average	1 hour 24 hours 1 year
15	Suspended particulate matter	micrograms of suspended particulate matter per cubic metre of air	90 average 60 geometric mean	24 hours 1 year

Ontario Regulation 374/70: Sulphur Content of Fuels

INTERPRETATION

1. In this Regulation,

   (*a*) "fuel" includes any fuel used for heating, generating steam or electricity, or for industrial processes;

   (*b*) "sulphur content" means the amount of sulphur in the fuel as determined by standard methods of sampling and testing and in the case of coal shall be determined as organic sulphur.

APPLICATION

2. This Regulation applies to The Municipality of Metropolitan Toronto.

3. Subject to section 4, no person shall use for fuel, or sell or offer for sale, any fuel referred to in column 1 of the Schedule if the sulphur content of the fuel is greater than the maximum sulphur content set opposite thereto,

   (*a*) in column 2 of the Schedule, from and including the 1st day of January in the year 1971 to and including the 31st day of December in the year 1971;

   (*b*) in column 3 of the Schedule, from and including the 1st day of January in the year 1972 to and including the 31st day of December in the year 1972; and

   (*c*) in column 4 of the Schedule, from and including the 1st day of January in the year 1973 to and including the 31st day of December, 1973.

4. A fuel having a higher sulphur content than the maximum sulphur content prescribed for that fuel in the Schedule may be used for fuel, or sold or offered for sale to a purchaser if the user or purchaser has applied for and obtained a certificate of approval, under section 7 of the Act, for methods or devices that will result in emissions of sulphur dioxide no greater than if the fuel contained the sulphur content prescribed in the Schedule.

5. The standard methods to be used for sampling and testing fuels for sulphur content shall be submitted to the Air Management Branch

of the Department for approval prior to the 1st day of December, 1970.

6. Every supplier of fuel,
    (*a*) shall report to the Air Management Branch of the Department the sulphur content of the fuels supplied by him; and
    (*b*) shall specify to the Air Management Branch of the Department the source or sources of supply of the fuels supplied by him, at such times and in such manner as the Air Management Branch of the Department specifies.

7. Every supplier of fuel shall, upon the request of a provincial officer, provide duplicate samples of any fuel supplied by him.

SCHEDULE

	COLUMN 1	COLUMN 2	COLUMN 3	COLUMN 4
Fuel	Grade or type of Fuel	Maximum Sulphur Content	Maximum Sulphur Content	Maximum Sulphur Content
Oil	1	0.5%	0.5%	0.5%
	2	0.5%	0.5%	0.5%
	4	1.5%	1.5%	1.5%
	5	1.9%	1.75%	1.5%
	6B	2.0%	1.75%	1.5%
	6C	2.0%	1.75%	1.5%
Coal	Bituminous	2.0%	1.75%	1.5%